LEADING PROJECT
TEAMS

Anthony T. Cobb
Virginia Tech

LEADING PROJECT
TEAMS

An Introduction to the Basics of Project Management and Project Team Leadership

SAGE Publications
Thousand Oaks ▪ London ▪ New Delhi

For information:

Sage Publications, Inc.
2455 Teller Road
Thousand Oaks, California 91320
E-mail: order@sagepub.com

Sage Publications Ltd.
1 Oliver's Yard
55 City Road
London EC1Y 1SP
United Kingdom

Sage Publications India Pvt. Ltd.
B-42, Panchsheel Enclave
Post Box 4109
New Delhi 110 017 India

Printed in the United States of America

Library of Congress Cataloging-in-Publication Data

Cobb, Anthony T.
Leading project teams: An introduction to the basics of project management and project team leadership / Anthony T. Cobb.
      p. cm.
Includes index.
ISBN 1-4129-0947-3 (pbk.)
   1. Project management. 2. Teams in the workplace. I. Title.
HD69.P75C616 2006
658.4′022—dc22   2005022463

This book is printed on acid-free paper.

05   06   07   08   09   8   7   6   5   4   3   2   1

Acquisitions Editor:	Al Bruckner
Editorial Assistant:	MaryAnn Vail
Production Editor:	Diane S. Foster
Copy Editor:	Julie Gwin
Typesetter:	C&M Digitals (P) Ltd.
Proofreader:	Emily Rose
Indexer:	Molly Hall
Cover Designer:	Edgar Abarca

Contents

1. Introduction 1

2. Determining the Direction and Initial 13
   Specifications of a Project

3. The Work Breakdown Structure 37

4. Project Scheduling 59

5. Developing Project Teams 81

6. The Project Team's Environment 101

7. Leading Project Teams 119

8. Writing Project Reports 141

Appendix A: Calculating the Critical
Path Using the Critical Path Method 159

Appendix B: Earned Value Analysis 165

Index 173

About the Author 178

1

Introduction

Introduction	1
Project Fundamentals	3
Defining Characteristics of Projects	3
Projects Are Unique	3
Projects Are Temporary	4
Project Parameters	5
Dimensions of Project Leadership	5
Overview of Book	6
Chapters 2 to 4: Fundamentals of Project	
Initiation and Planning	6
Chapter 2: Determining the Direction	
and Initial Specifications of a Project	7
Chapter 3: The Work Breakdown Structure	7
Chapter 4: Project Scheduling	8
Chapters 5 to 7: Fundamentals of Project Leadership	8
Chapter 5: Developing Project Teams	8
Chapter 6: The Project Team's Environment	9
Chapter 7: Leading Project Teams	9
Chapter 8: Writing Project Reports	9
Summary	10
Endnotes	11

Interest in and demand for project management has increased a great deal over the past 15 years. This increase in interest and demand can be seen in a number of ways. One way is in the number of books oriented to project management, which now number in the thousands. Another is in the growth of training programs offered in project management that are now widely available and also number in the thousands.[1] Still a third way is in college recruiting. Recruiters often develop much more interest in students when they mention their project management training or their experience in leading project teams. Perhaps most indicative of interest in project management is the results one gets from "Googling" project management: more than 25 *million* hits![2]

Part of this increase in demand is due to growth in what can be called "traditional" project work. Most of the early work in project management was done by engineers working for large "performing" companies that conducted large-scale projects for outside clients.[3] Working on projects like high-rise construction or large weapon systems, these professionals developed most of the project management tools we now use. Certainly, demand for these kinds of projects has increased over the years.

Interest in project management, however, has grown in a number of other areas. One area is new product development. Product life cycles have shrunk a great deal as organizations have turned to new product development as a competitive strategy. To remain competitive, organizations have had to constantly update and remodel what they offer their customers. Companies have found that bringing new products to market is best managed in a project environment using cross-functional project teams.

Another area of growth is in the demand for new organizational processes. Organizations not only have to constantly develop new products to remain competitive, but they have to constantly develop themselves as well. From quality circles to "Tiger Teams," organizations have looked to project teams to reinvent and re-engineer themselves to attain ever-increasing levels of quality and efficiency.

These kinds of challenges have produced what might be called a "project mind-set." Whenever something of significance needs to be done—a problem solved or an opportunity seized—higher management assembles project teams to do the work. Whether the projects are making process improvements, starting new ventures, developing new client services, finding and opening new market niches, or even running political campaigns, leaders have come to value project management tools and skills in planning and conducting them.

With this broadening of project work, the composition of project teams has also changed. Although many are still composed of builders or engineers, most are not. Members come from all walks of life and from all professions.

Project teams are assembled on the shop floor; in laboratories, universities, government offices, and school districts; and in the executive suite, to name just a few project "work sites."

The level of skills required for these project teams has also changed. Although the full range of skills used by professional project engineers is always useful, most of the need is for more entry-level project skills. Smaller projects depend less on sophisticated tools to do such tasks as cost or risk analysis and depend much more on tools needed to organize projects, clarify deliverables, work with stakeholders, and manage and lead project teams.

This book is written to help convey entry-level project tools and skills for the newcomer to project management. It is designed so it can be used as a supplemental text in courses dedicated to topics other than project management. In these kinds of venues, its aims are twofold. First, it aims to help student teams become more effective at doing course projects by learning project management techniques and applying them to their work. Teams are simply more effective and learn more when they have the skills to do the course's projects well. Second, it aims to help prepare students to enter the kind of "project life" that has come to dominate so much of modern organizational work. From whatever area of study students emerge, recruiters see project training and experience as value added, and this gives the student a comparative advantage over those who have not benefited from such training.

In the remainder of this chapter, we examine some of the fundamental notions of what characterizes projects and what makes them unique. We then turn our attention to how the basic tools of project management are addressed in this book as well as essential elements of successful project leadership.

Project Fundamentals

Defining Characteristics of Projects

The Project Management Institute defines a *project* as a temporary endeavor undertaken to create a unique product, service, or result.[4] The two defining characteristics of projects, then, are that they are unique and temporary.

Projects Are Unique

Projects are unique in terms of the outcomes they produce. Just how unique they are, however, can vary a great deal. At one extreme, we might find the development of new weapons systems. They may require yet-to-be-developed composites for armor, space-age munitions, cutting-edge guidance systems, and the like. Most projects, however, produce products and services far less exotic. Custom-built homes, for example, are unique from one another but similar in other respects: basics of foundations, wiring, plumbing, and the like. When a company opens a new market area, it is likely producing a unique outcome although the company may have opened many others in the past—each new one is likely different in some significant way from all the others. Although these projects may not present the design challenges of a new weapons system, those who lead them know how challenging they are.

This leads us to another aspect of what makes projects unique. They are unique in terms of how they are conducted. They are unique in terms of their staffing, their stakeholders, the resources used, when things have to be done, how work is to be coordinated, and a host of other operational aspects.

It is because organizations face these kinds of challenges on an almost daily basis that project management tools and skills have become so much in demand. There is little doubt that these tools and skills can help with these kinds of projects. How they are used to plan and control a project, however, is always a problem-solving process, and each new project has to be hand crafted.

Projects Are Temporary

Projects are also temporary endeavors. They have a life cycle that fundamentally affects their structure, dynamics, and operations, and, as a result, their management. Project life cycles have been described in a number of ways, but we will focus on five stages: initiation, planning, launch, execution, and closing.[5] *Initiation* is the stage in which a project's key stakeholders first come together to define the broad outlines of a project. A key objective of this stage is to come to a common understanding of what the project is supposed to produce and estimate what it will take to do so. Given this understanding and these estimates, another key objective is to decide whether to move forward with the project.

In organizations dedicated to project work, the initiation phase results in an assessment of whether a project fits with the organization's profit goals or business model. We examine it here in a more general way—to make sure significant stakeholders are on board before moving too far down the road.

The *planning stage* emerges once a decision is made to move forward. Here, more detailed planning is done to "nail down" a wide range of project specifics, including the precise tasks required to produce the project's products and services, more precise estimates of resource needs and their costs, and the time required to perform project work. In addition, how project tasks will be arranged across the project's life cycle will be determined and mapped onto a project schedule. These come together in a project plan—a blueprint—of what the project will look like, and the plan is used in the actual conduct of the project. This plan, too, needs to be approved by significant stakeholders before major project work actually begins.

The *launch* of a project is done once the planning is complete and initial resources are committed. Beginning the actual work on a project is a critical juncture in any project's life and demands a great deal of leader attention. Not the least of this attention is aimed at assembling the right project team, structuring the team so that it can reach its potential, and correctly initiating its project work.

The major objective of the *execution stage* is to keep the project on track once it has been launched. Working with the project team, leaders need to control the pace of project work, its costs, and performance quality. Working with external stakeholders, leaders need to maintain project support, ensure flow of project resources, and minimize but adapt to project pressures, disruptions, and changes.

Finally, projects enter the *closing* phase. In this phase, final products, services, and other project outcomes are delivered to the client. Project ties to the performing or host organization are retired and the project team itself disbands. Each of these activities requires proper managerial and leadership attention.

Project Parameters

There are three major parameters to every project: scope, costs, and time. *Project scope* refers to the sum total of all work to be done to produce the project's deliverables—the products and services to be delivered to the customer. *Costs* are the sum total of project costs to do the project's work. Finally, *time* is the amount of time given to complete the project.

These parameters are closely linked. If the project's scope of work changes to accommodate a change in deliverables, for example, costs and time are affected. If a project is given more time, on the other hand, work might consume fewer resources, resulting in lower cost. Costs generally increase, however, when the time given to do the project is shortened. Close attention needs to be given to each of these areas from the very beginning of a project through its execution.

Dimensions of Project Leadership

Although there are many dimensions of leadership, the literature has traditionally focused on two: the task and social-psychological dimensions. Traditional project management attends well to the task side of project leadership. Project tools help leaders do a variety of task work, including clarifying the project's mission and objectives; planning, organizing, and structuring project work; coordinating the flow of resources and task outputs; and controlling the operational side of project work.

The social-psychological dimension of leadership focuses on how leaders operate in the social context and in one-on-one relationships that surround and support task work. Much of this literature focuses on leader-subordinate relationships and is relevant to working with the project team. Among other things, leaders need to staff, develop, motivate, and ensure commitment from their project teams.

Project leaders must also attend to the broader social context in which their projects reside. Leaders need to identify and work with their key project stakeholders, taking into account their interests and needs. Project leaders bridge the gap between their teams and the project's other stakeholders. Being the key liaison between these two worlds, leaders must be able to communicate effectively with both team members and stakeholders. They must negotiate agreement between and among them, solve personal and political as well as technical problems, and maintain support and commitment to the project from all parties, to name just a few job responsibilities. Faced with challenges such as these, it is not surprising that many project leaders wish all they had to worry about was the task side of projects, no matter how complicated and complex they may be.

This book is oriented to these kinds of issues. In the first part, the task side of project leadership is given primary attention. Project management tools are presented and discussed in terms of how they are used by project leaders. In the second part of the book, leadership issues come to the forefront. We focus on the team, the project's stakeholders, and the leader him- or herself. A final chapter is devoted to project reports.

Overview of Book

This book is divided into two major sections. The first focuses on tools leaders use in project initiation and planning. The second section focuses on the human resources of project leadership and includes attention to writing up project reports.

Chapters 2 to 4: Fundamentals of Project Initiation and Planning

Chapters 2 to 4 are devoted to project initiation and planning. Although technical issues receive the most attention, managerial and leadership issues are also discussed. The purpose of this section is to help the reader develop an entry-level understanding of these project management tools and how project leaders use them.

Chapter 2: Determining the Direction and Initial Specifications of a Project

This chapter is designed to help new project leaders sort out what to do when they are first approached about a project and the steps they need to take to initiate it. The objective of project initiation is to assemble the basic information needed to assess the basic parameters of a project. This information is shared with the project's stakeholders so that adjustments and decisions can be made whether to move ahead with a project and, if so, what will be needed for a project's successful completion.

We begin by discussing the project's basic mission statement and how to identify those who have an important stake in the project. Properly constructed, mission statements provide a common understanding of—and agreement about—the project's ultimate purpose among project stakeholders.

Next, we examine how to refine the project's broad mission into concrete deliverables—the products, services, and other outcomes the project is responsible for producing. Project deliverables nail down exactly what a project is supposed to produce and provide the basis for project planning and execution.

Third, we discuss developing good early estimates of a project's resource, cost, and time requirements. Before a project moves too far forward, relevant stakeholders need a good estimate of these requirements and must agree to them.

Finally, we discuss the need to develop a project charter so all relevant stakeholders can review and sign off on it. The project charter lays out all the important parameters of the project in one document. Project leaders need to develop a common understanding among key stakeholders about the important aspects of a project and agreement to provide the resources necessary before the project moves too far. The project's charter serves that purpose. We wrap up this chapter by laying out some of the essential elements of the project's plan—the blueprint of the project that will be developed over the next few chapters.

Chapter 3: The Work Breakdown Structure

The operational foundation of any project is the scope of work needed to produce its deliverables. The work breakdown structure helps create that foundation by detailing all the tasks needed in a project. This chapter reviews what work breakdown structures are, how they are developed, and how they are used in project planning, organization, and control.

We examine first what a work breakdown structure is and the various roles it plays in project planning and control. We go on to discuss how work breakdown structures are developed, focusing on both core and support tasks in the project. Finally, we discuss how work breakdown structures are used to estimate project resources, timelines, and costs. We attend as well to how work breakdown structures can be used to develop the project's organizational structure.

Chapter 4: Project Scheduling

Project schedules arrange when project tasks are to be done across the project's life cycle. The project schedule is a principal managerial tool used to organize, coordinate, and control project work.

First, we review three common scheduling tools and how they are used. Next, we discuss the basic components of any project schedule and their uses. We then focus on the Gantt or bar chart and discuss how to construct it. Finally, we discuss the various ways project leaders can use schedules to plan, organize, and control a project.

Chapters 5 to 7: Fundamentals of Project Leadership

Project leadership requires working effectively with two groups of project participants: the project team and external project stakeholders. In Chapter 5, we examine how best to construct and develop project teams to do project work. In Chapter 6, we identify who stakeholders are, their differing interests, and some ways to work with them. Chapter 7 focuses on project leadership per se.

Chapter 5: Developing Project Teams

Project teams are the key resource leaders use in any project. This chapter is designed to help project leaders understand how teams are best constructed and developed. We cover first what a team is and what constitutes team success. We then turn attention to those elements of a team's structure that can help or hinder its success. Team factors covered include team size, composition, governance, identity, interactions, and ideology. These factors need to be given attention in the construction of a team and its development.

We end by discussing the developmental stages groups go through on their way to becoming truly effective teams: forming, storming, norming, performing, and adjourning. We discuss the characteristics of each stage and, importantly, what teams need from their leaders to be effective and to progress further in their development.

Chapter 6: The Project Team's Environment

Projects operate in an environment of stakeholders who will influence and likely determine project success. Leaders need to work in this environment to make sure the project gets the support and resources it needs to complete its work. This chapter identifies the characteristics and needs of a project's principal stakeholders and how to work effectively in the project's stakeholder network.

We begin by identifying some of the more important project stakeholders and provide suggestions about how best to work with them. Project leaders play a key liaison role in tying these stakeholders together and to the project. Properly used, this liaison role can provide the leader with the social capital he or she needs to acquire critical project resources and support. We examine social capital in this chapter and how project leaders can develop and use it.

Chapter 7: Leading Project Teams

Project leaders are expected to play a number of roles in any project. We review those roles and the expectations that come with them, and we offer suggestions about how best to address them. Projects need different things from their leaders at different stages in their life cycle. We address those needs and how to meet them during project initiation and planning, project launch, execution, and, finally, project closing. Finally, we discuss how project leaders can best lead individual project members to develop their value to the project.

Chapter 8: Writing Project Reports

Projects often require a number of reports to be produced at various times in their life cycles. We focus on the final, formal project report to address issues important to any project report. Writing effective reports requires knowledge of who will read them and what they are looking for in project reports. We begin by identifying some of the more important readers of project reports and how best to address their needs. We then turn our attention to the report itself. Our approach is to walk through the final project report and discuss how different sections of the report should be written. We start with the front end, addressing such elements as the cover page, table of contents, and, most important, the executive summary. We then turn attention to the body of the report, covering introductions, major sections and subsections, conclusions and recommendations, and references. We finish up with a discussion of supporting appendices. At each juncture, we discuss basic elements of the section and how to address the needs of different readers.

Summary

Interest in project management has increased dramatically over the past 15 years. Much of this increase can be attributed to increased demand for more traditional projects conducted by larger construction and engineering firms. Most of the increase, however, has come from smaller scale projects aimed at different missions, staffed by a wider range of project personnel, and often conducted by organizations for themselves. Although sophisticated project management skills and tools are always useful, these kinds of smaller projects have increased the demand for what might be called a more entry-level skill set. This book is addressed to those skills and tools.

Projects are temporary endeavors undertaken to create unique products, services, or other outcomes. Projects are unique not only in the outcomes they produce but in the design and operation of the projects themselves. Each project is, to some extent, hand crafted, and leaders need to learn the basic tools to do the work anew with each new project. Projects are also temporary endeavors that have a life cycle that deeply affects project operations and leadership requirements. The stages of a project can be broken out into initiation, planning, launch, execution, and closing. Each stage has its own objectives and needs to which leaders must attend.

All projects have three basic parameters: scope, cost, and time. Project scope is the sum total of tasks needed to produce the products and services of a project—its deliverables. The costs of a project are all related costs that are expended in doing project work. Time is the time given to the project to complete its work. These three parameters are connected so that increases or decreases in one will affect one or more of the others.

Two basic dimensions of leadership are explored in this book: the task and social-psychological sides of leadership. The task dimension focuses on what is needed to get the task done. Project management tools and techniques go a long way toward addressing these needs. The first part of this book focuses on this aspect of project leadership: project direction and specification, the work breakdown structure, and project schedules.

The social-psychological dimension focuses on how leaders operate in the broader social and personal context of the project. The second part of this book deals with addressing these needs: constructing and developing teams, identifying and dealing with project stakeholders, exploring the leadership role, and communicating with stakeholders through project reports.

Endnotes

1. This number comes from the results of an Internet search of "training project management" on November 12, 2004.

2. Google search of "project management" on November 12, 2004.

3. Those who pay for getting project work done are called by various names. The term *client* is often used in the consulting industry. *Customer* is used most often by organizations that do work for the federal government. The Project Management Institute equates "customer" with the end user of the project's output—those, for example, who would fly and travel on an airplane developed for an airline. The terms *client* and *customer* are used interchangeably here with *end user*, specifying those who will actually use the output of a project.

4. The Project Management Institute. (2000). *Guide to the project management body of knowledge.* Newtown Square, PA: Author.

5. These labels are taken in large part from what the Project Management Institute (2000) characterized as the basic processes that occur in different project phases: initiating, planning, executing, controlling, and closing. Here, "executing" refers to the actual conduct of the project, which includes controlling processes. "Launch" is added to give special focus to the initial process of assembling resources and kicking off the project. This short but critical stage requires the undivided attention of project leaders.

2

Determining the Direction and Initial Specifications of a Project

Introduction	14
The Baltimore Project	14
Chapter Overview	15
The Project's Mission Statement	16
What Is a Project Mission Statement and	
What Role Does It Play?	16
Project Direction	16
The "Political" Role	17
Stakeholders in the Project's Mission	17
The Client	17
The Host Organization	17
The Project Team	18
End Users	18
Suppliers	18
Dealing With Stakeholders	19
The Baltimore Project	19
The Project's Objectives and Deliverables	20
What Are Project Objectives and Deliverables?	21
Roles Played by Project's	
Objectives and Deliverables	21

Helping the Client	21
Providing Team Direction	21
Securing Stakeholder Agreement	22
The Baltimore Project	22
Project Parameters: Scope, Costs, and Timeline	25
Scope	25
Costs	27
Timeline	27
Developing and Signing Off on the Project's Charter	28
The Project Plan	30
Summary	31
Review Questions	33
Exercise	33
Endnotes	34
Figure 2.1: Talking Points for the Meeting With Ms. Byrne	24
Table 2.1: Illustration of John's Mission Statement, a Project Objective, and Its Deliverables	23
Table 2.2: Initiation Check-Off List	29

Introduction

The Baltimore Project

John had no idea what was coming when he picked up his phone early one Monday morning at work—the corporate offices of Acme Auto Supply. Acme Auto was a mid-sized company that grossed more than $500 million in revenues last year and was gaining a reputation on Wall Street as an aggressive and growing company.

"Hey, John, you got a minute? I'd like to chat with you about a job I have in mind." It was Carol Byrnes, the director of John's division. Ten minutes later, John was getting comfortable in Carol's office and wondering what was on her mind. "You know, John, we are opening our new store in Baltimore come June 15th." "Yes, Ms. Byrnes, I do know; guess it's going to be some event!" "Well, that's right," Carol said. "That's why I called you. It's important that we open the store well because it is our first entry in this new market area. In fact, we want this opening to exceed any of our others. The brass is looking to see how well the store starts out to determine the extent and pace of rolling out all our other planned stores in the Northeast corridor." "Guess that makes sense," John replied, trying to figure out why Carol was telling him all this.

"Well, John, I'd like you to take on the opening. I've talked to Ralph [John's boss] and a few other division folks, and we all are agreed you can handle this project. It means a lot to the organization and a lot to us in the division. If all goes well, it can mean a lot to you as well. Ralph can clear your plate of the Carlisle account, and we can give you Tom and, maybe, Alice to help. Can you run with this?"

What else could he say? "Sure, I'd love the opportunity." "Great!" Carol replied. "You'll need to draw up some plans for the 'Baltimore Project' and I'll want to review them, but let's have an initial talk tomorrow to see what you have come up with by then." Carol looked at her calendar. "Let's see, hmm, how about 3:00 tomorrow for an initial run through? I've got a half-hour slot open." "I'll see you at your office at 3:00, then," John replied, already beginning to get nervous about a high-visibility project dumped in his lap that he knew little to nothing about and that was only 6 weeks away from completion.

Chapter Overview

New projects can provoke more than a little anxiety even for those who deal with them often. This particular one is more than likely to do so. It is a high-visibility project, John has never opened a store before, and he has no idea how to get started. On top of it all, John wants to look good tomorrow for his meeting with Ms. Byrnes.

When any client brings a project to a project leader, the leader needs to develop an initial overview plan of the project: to determine what it is trying to achieve, who the important stakeholders are, and rough estimates of the work, cost, time, and other requirements of the project. Once done, the leader needs to review the project's initial plan with the key principals involved and get their commitment to it. Preparing for this task is John's job for his next meeting with Carol. The steps John needs to take are the subject of this chapter.

We begin by examining the project's mission and some of the stakeholders who have an interest in it. We then focus attention on the project's more concrete objectives and its deliverables. Next, we address some of the other components of any project—its scope, resource, time, and cost estimates. These are brought together in the project's charter—the initial overview of a project's plan to be approved by the leader's superiors. We wrap things up by pointing out the other elements needed in a full project plan.

The Project's Mission Statement

All projects have a mission. That mission is to help address some need or solve some problem for a client. Constructing a formal mission statement helps leaders to understand and clarify the broader aims of a project, and mission statements themselves play a number of useful roles in it. Writing a mission statement is the first step project leaders need to take.

As a project leader begins to organize the project around its mission, it is important as well to identify the important stakeholders of the project—those who have an interest in it and can deeply affect it in some way. Who those stakeholders are, and what interests they have in the project, are important determinates of any project's success or failure.

What Is a Project Mission Statement and What Role Does It Play?

A mission statement states the purpose of a project—its general direction and aims. In a few sentences or paragraphs, it states what the project and its sponsoring clients are trying to achieve. Mission statements play a number of roles in a project, but two are very important. The first is that a mission statement helps establish and maintain the project's overall direction. The second is that it can play a useful "political" role.

Project Direction

Many different people play different roles and make different contributions in a project. All those roles and contributions are supposed to fit together in some way to produce what the project is supposed to deliver. Mission statements help tie all these contributions together. In managerial terms, a mission statement helps provide unity of purpose and unity of effort in the project. It does so by clarifying the project's goals and requirements.

When a project team is first assembled, for example, the mission statement provides a common orientation to the project and its direction. As work is broken down and assigned, members can see how their efforts contribute to the project's mission as a whole. As a project moves forward, project members quite often work at different locations and narrow their project focus to their own particular jobs. The project's mission statement can help team members make sure their efforts will contribute to the ultimate aims of the project.

In a similar manner, those external to the project's team can assess their contributions in terms of the project's mission. Mission statements provide suppliers, consultants, regulators, and others with a common idea of the aims of a project and how their contributions fit into it.

The "Political" Role

When mission statements are designed with the principal stakeholders' advice and consent, they become a common declaration of their common aim. As such, they provide common ground for those stakeholders' interests. That common ground can be used throughout the project to keep stakeholder ties strong. When unforeseen events arise calling for project changes, for example, the interests of different stakeholders may come into conflict. Mission statements help the principal stakeholders to keep their "eyes on the prize"—the project's mission—when events may require change. During such times, the broader aims of a mission statement can provide a common "venue" where stakeholders can negotiate in good faith.

Stakeholders in the Project's Mission

Any project will have a number of stakeholders who have vested interests in its mission and how it will be achieved. Success or failure of a project often turns on how well project leaders identify and work with these critical project stakeholders.

Important stakeholders in any project include the clients of the project and the host or performing organization in which the project is being done. The project team is an important stakeholder, as are the end users and various resource suppliers.

The Client

The project's client is the reason a project exists. Every project is designed to address some need brought by a client, and the client is the ultimate source of resources for the project. Clients' interests lie in having their needs met as much as possible, as quickly as possible, and, generally, for as low a price as possible.

The Host Organization

The host or performing organization[1] is the organization in which the project is conducted. The traditional model is that clients come to an organization to serve their needs. The organization, in turn, assembles project teams to do so. The interests of host organizations include making a profit from the endeavor and keeping the project and other parts of the organization running smoothly.

Organizations quite often undertake projects for their own purposes. Developing a new car model, for example, is a rather large project conducted periodically by automobile companies. Opening new markets (like John is helping to do), developing new products and services, conducting comprehensive studies of some aspect of an organization, and designing and leading organizational change are other common examples of projects conducted by organizations for their own benefit.[2] When organizations embark on such endeavors, project leaders are dealing with a stakeholder who is a client as well as the host organization.

The Project Team

The project team is a critical stakeholder of any project, and the project leader will do well to look out for its interests even before it is assembled. Although project teams have many interests, an overriding one is simply to be able to do the project, given the time and cost constraints and the products and services to be delivered. Other key interests are to have a smoothly running project with minimum disruption from changes and having the resources to do the job when they are needed.

End Users

End users are those ultimately intended to use or benefit from a project. Their interests focus on the utility of what is produced for them. The end users of the Baltimore Project, for example, are the intended customers of the Baltimore store. The gala opening will be successful only to the extent that potential customers are attracted to it. This, in turn, affects decisions about what kinds of advertising to use and the promotional incentives offered.

Suppliers

Projects often need suppliers to deliver the products and services that the team itself cannot supply. The interests of outside suppliers include increasing their revenues by servicing the project. Often, their interests focus more on revenues than on other issues. Projects may also have internal suppliers in the host organization who are called on to help supply information, personnel, space, equipment, and the like. Quite often, the costs of these resources are not reimbursed. As one might imagine, this can set up a supplier/project relationship far different from one in which an outside supplier is paid for products and services.

Dealing With Stakeholders

We have identified a number of stakeholder categories and will explore them and others much more in Chapter 6, as well as how best to work with them. For now, however, project leaders should remember that they never deal with clients, higher management, suppliers, and the like. They deal with the people who represent them or play their roles, and project leaders need to consider carefully their interests and concerns. In addition, leaders need to be aware of who the key players in those stakeholder categories are. Key players are those who have the power and authority to make important decisions about the conduct and outcomes of the project. Although all stakeholders should command attention and respect, key players require extra time and attention.

As project leaders work through their mission statements and progress through the scoping of a project, they need to keep the principal stakeholders of the project in mind. These stakeholders often have conflicting interests that must be reconciled for the project to be a success. Although always a challenge, addressing those interests is far easier to do earlier in the project than later.

The Baltimore Project

It should not take John long to develop a workable mission statement for his project. A thoughtful review of those affected by the project will also point to its principal stakeholders. As a beginning, John's mission statement might state:

> The Baltimore opening is to be a gala event designed to attract Acme's principal customer base to view the products and services offered by the Baltimore store. The event will occur on or about June 15th.[3]

The stakeholders of this project include Ms. Byrnes and "the brass" in the host organization, who also play the role of clients of the project. Ralph, John's immediate supervisor, is an important stakeholder as well. Other stakeholders include the manager of the Baltimore store and the end users the event is supposed to attract: the potential retail and business customers of the store. The project team includes John as project leader and both Tom and Alice as project members who were "volunteered" by Ms. Byrnes. Someone at the Baltimore store might also be recruited to play a role on the project team.

As the project moves forward, vendors will be added to the stakeholder list who will supply advertising for the opening (e.g., newspapers, radio) and supplies for the store itself as the site for the opening's events (e.g., caterers, performers, store suppliers demonstrating their products).

John has laid out the general direction of the project and identified some of its key stakeholders. John needs to turn his attention now to the more specific objectives of the project and the specific products and services his project will provide—its deliverables.

The Project's Objectives and Deliverables

A few years ago, I was teaching a master's in business administration class on the basics of project management when an interesting event occurred. Project teams were presenting project proposals to other class teams, who were acting in the role of clients. The project leader of one team had finished presenting her team's proposal when she started to be questioned quite aggressively by one of the more experienced students. "Would the project turn in quality product, at cost, on schedule?" demanded the client. "Of course!" responded the project lead. "Will you guarantee satisfaction with the product?" After thinking for a moment, the project leader said, "Of course." At that point, the client turned to the instructor and simply smiled—he had forced the project leader into an impossible position. No matter what was produced, it need not be "satisfactory" in the eyes of the client. At every step of the project, the client could easily make demands on the project with the threat that it was not proceeding in a satisfactory manner.

At least two important lessons were learned that day. First, stakeholders have interests of their own that they pursue—sometimes very aggressively. Even if a stakeholder is not adversarial, honest disagreements can arise, and they usually come up "down the road" in projects, when things are tough to change. The second lesson was that although client satisfaction is always paramount, just what *will* satisfy a client should be hammered out before the project gets under way. "Of course," the project lead might have replied, "and we will work very closely with you in the planning process to specify what exactly will satisfy your needs before we begin the project."

Every project leader is faced with this same problem: What exactly can be done to satisfy the client—and can it be done on schedule and on budget? Once the general direction is given by the mission statement, the project's more specific objectives and deliverables need to be developed to help answer these questions.

What Are Project Objectives and Deliverables?

The project's objectives are those objectives a project must achieve to fulfill its mission. John's project, for example, will likely have a number of project objectives. One set of objectives will likely focus on the event itself— what it is trying to accomplish. Another set of project objectives will likely focus on just who should be coming to the event and how many of them— the market segments of the store's potential customers.

The project's deliverables are the specific products and services produced to achieve those objectives. Project deliverables include interim as well as final deliverables.[4] Once these deliverables are provided, the project's mission is complete—the job is done. For example, making sure the right kinds of customers show up will likely be one objective of John's project. Specific deliverables might include using some mix of targeted advertising and promotional incentives to accomplish that objective. Interim deliverables might include specific reports to Ms. Byrnes and options for various activities that she will need to approve for the event itself.

Roles Played by Project's Objectives and Deliverables

Project objectives and deliverables play a variety of roles in a project. One is that they help clients see their project in concrete terms. Another is that they provide the project team with specific outcomes to achieve. Still a third role is that they force stakeholders to make hard choices and trade-offs as they pursue their interests.

Helping the Client

When clients first present their projects—their needs, problems, goals, and ideas—they are often ambiguous at best. Developing a mission statement is an important first step in clarifying their aims. The process of developing project objectives and their deliverables moves the project forward another important step. It helps clients think through exactly what will address their needs given their resource and time constraints. Helping clients "operationalize" their aims in concrete, "doable" terms is one of the most important services project leaders can provide.[5]

Providing Team Direction

Project objectives and deliverables also play an important role for the project team. Once specified, they can be translated into specific tasks needed to

achieve them. These, in turn, provide the task objectives needed to direct individual and team efforts. Specificity is the key here, and the best objectives are SMART. They are Specific and Measurable. They are also Actionable—suggestive of the actions needed to achieve them—and Realistic—achievable even if challenging. Finally, they are Time delimited; they have a time frame within which they are to be achieved.[6]

Securing Stakeholder Agreement

Developing a project's objectives and deliverables also forces stakeholders to confront and work through their different interests. Projects often have a number of clients, for example, and each can have their own desires and interests. In John's project, Ms. Byrnes and the store manager are clients who are likely to have different desires and needs. In addition, clients will have different interests than host organizations, and project teams will have their own concerns as well. Developing a common set of project objectives and deliverables sets up a process by which different stakeholders must negotiate their interests to arrive at a specific set of concrete project outcomes. Confronting the hard choices in a project needs to be done earlier rather than later in a project, when adjustments are more difficult or impossible to make.[7]

The Baltimore Project

As stated earlier, John's project calls for at least two sets of project objectives. The first focuses on promotion—how to get potential customers to the store's grand opening. The second focuses on venue—what to do with the customers once they arrive.

With regard to promotions, Acme Auto Supply sells to both the retail "do-it-yourself" customer and to professional auto mechanics. One project objective might be to reach 80% of the general population within a 10-mile radius of the store, notifying them of the store's opening, the opening events, and any other promotional offerings (e.g., store coupons). Another objective might be to notify 99+% of all auto repair shops within a 15-mile radius about the store's opening, opening events of special interest to them, special services the store will offer to professional mechanics, and any special promotional offers targeting them.

Given these objectives, project deliverables need to be developed to target those customers. Specific advertising and promotional incentives need to be designed, for example, that would interest them. In addition, radio, local television, print media, and direct mailings are all possible deliverables that need to be considered for getting the message out.

With regard to the venue, project objectives might focus on what sorts of events are to take place at the store during the opening and what sorts of ancillaries are needed—refreshments, props, local celebrities, and the like. Project objectives here might include providing refreshments for all attendees during the event; providing promotional signs, games, and other similar attractions for the general public; and providing special refreshments, displays, and demonstrations to all professional mechanics who attend the event. Project deliverables will make explicit just what must be delivered to achieve these objectives.

Importantly, John will need to work closely with the store manager in this project. The store manager is a principal stakeholder with whom John will need to clarify promotional and venue needs. Venue objectives and deliverables will need particular attention in this regard. Just who will provide what services will require constructive negotiation with an eye toward yet another mission: to make the launch of the new store a financial success. An example of John's project mission and some of its objectives and possible deliverables is given in Table 2.1.

Table 2.1   Illustration of John's Mission Statement, a Project Objective, and Its Deliverables

---

- **Project mission:** The mission of this project is to develop and stage the opening of the new Baltimore store. The opening is to be a gala event designed to attract Acme's principal customer base to view the products and services offered by the store. The event will occur on or about June 15th.

- **Project objective:** The project's advertising will reach at least 80% of the general population within a 10-mile radius of the store, notifying them of the store's opening, the opening events, and any other promotional offerings. The project will also notify 99+% of all auto repair shops within a 15-mile radius of the store about the store's opening, opening events of special interest to them, special services the store will offer to professional mechanics, and any special promotional offers targeting them.

- **Project deliverables**

- **General population:** Newspaper copy will advertise the opening of the store every day for a week prior to its opening. The copy will include a description of the event and coupons for promotional items (to be determined by store manager). Radio spots will be given about the store, its grand opening, and sale items (to be determined by store manager) on three of the area's most listened-to stations. These will include three spots per hour between 8 A.M. and 7 P.M. for three days prior to the grand opening.

(Continued)

Table 2.1 (Continued)

- **Business customers:** Direct mailings to all auto repair shops within the specified radius of the store will be made one week before opening. In addition to information about the opening, several promotional items will be given to those who show up (to be determined by store manager). Personal visits by team members will be made to all auto repair shops with more than 10 mechanics within that radius. Phone invitations will be made to all auto repair shops with between four and nine mechanics. Additional promotional incentives will be given to mechanics and managers of these businesses (to be determined by store manager).

John will need to bring these ideas to his chief organizational client, Carol Byrnes, and begin the process of specifying exactly what the project will produce for the company. Working with Ms. Byrnes to clarify what the project will deliver is his all-important first step. As said earlier, John will need to work with the store manager closely and will need to work with a wide range of outside suppliers (e.g., the print media, mass mailers, and caterers) about what is doable and associated costs. Of course, John will need to keep in close communication with his direct supervisor, Ralph, about his need for time to work on the project and to keep Ralph generally informed about project progress. Finally, John would do well to identify and contact others who have opened stores in the past. Although this opening is to be unlike any other, consulting with them to explore action areas, deliverables, and what is achievable, and to get any "words of wisdom," will likely yield a great deal of useful information. These plans, too, he will share with Carol Byrnes in her role as a principal stakeholder in the host organization. Finally, in the hours before his meeting with Ms. Byrnes, John might make a few phone calls to see if he can get some early figures and information to bring to his meeting. A listing of key talking points for that meeting is given in Figure 2.1. Some of those points also touch on needed project resources and costs, and the project's timeline—the topics we consider next.

- Mission statement
  - Project objectives (action areas)
    - Venue
      Held at the store. What would Ms. Byrnes like to see included?
    - Advertising
      Several outlets possible (direct mail, radio, TV, newspaper, etc.).
      Any preferences?
    - Other?
      Any other action areas/project objectives that need attention?

Figure 2.1   Talking Points for the Meeting With Ms. Byrnes   *(Continued)*

- Stakeholders
  - Ralph (talk with prior to meeting to discuss any issues)
  - Ms. Byrnes as client and host sponsor
    Explore the components of a successful opening
    Any strategic and tactical advice on conducting the project?
    Any other managers I need to touch base with?
  - Project team
    How much of Tom's and Alice's time can be devoted to the project?
    What are their backgrounds?
    When can they start?
    Who do I need to work with to OK their work with me?
  - Store manager
    Will need to work closely with him or her. Plan to contact soon.
    What is standard practice in these kinds of working relationships?
    Any advice?
  - Others?
    Who else do I need to work with?
- Budget
  - Cost figures: Will develop based on similar openings. Does Ms.
    Byrnes have a figure in mind (keep options open)?
  - Other issues?
- Timeline
  - Possible effects on deliverables (e.g., venue and advertising)
  - Other issues?
- Other resource issues
  - Previous project leaders (who can I contact?)
  - Authority/support (from Ms. Byrnes within organization). Who needs
    to be notified of the project and me as its leader?
    Can I come to you if I need someone to "run interference"?

Figure 2.1   Talking Points for the Meeting With Ms. Byrnes

Project Parameters: Scope, Costs, and Timeline

The project's mission statement and objectives address what the project is trying to achieve. The deliverables address the products and services that will be produced toward those ends. Three other basic elements now require attention: the project's scope and the resources it will take to produce those deliverables, what they will cost, and how long it will take.

Scope

The project's scope includes all those tasks necessary to produce the deliverables required. A final project plan will detail those tasks, but at this stage, some basic estimates can direct our attention to the work that will be required and the resources needed to support that work. Resources related to both promotional and venue objectives, for example, will affect the costs of John's project. Estimates of these certainly need to be made. Three other kinds of resources also require attention, however, in ways that are often overlooked. These include human resources, information, and authority.

Human resources—the project team—are needed, of course, to work on the project's activities. Beyond personnel costs, however, project leaders need to consider the knowledge, skills, and abilities needed to perform work on the project and just who possesses them. Good human resources are notoriously in short supply, and the earlier project leaders can "lock them in," the better.

John's Baltimore project presents another, quite common issue with human resources. Members of his project team—Tom and Alice—were "volunteered" by Ms. Byrnes. When working with the store manager, John may find yet another person "volunteered" for his team. As early as possible, project leaders need to check out the knowledge, skills, and abilities of such resources as well as their true availability. When personnel are drawn from other parts of an organization, their time is usually committed to other projects. Both they and their supervisors are rarely happy to give *their* time to *your* project.[8]

Information is another often overlooked resource that needs to be acquired as soon as possible. Because projects are unique endeavors, information that can be helpful in planning and conducting them is invaluable. One excellent source of information is experience—one's own and that of others. Even before detailed planning begins, it serves leaders well to consider others who have experience in working on and leading projects similar to the one being considered. This would include potential team members, of course, but also others who might be able to shed some light on the project. Even a few "cold calls" can reap tremendous gains in information. Those who have labored in the "project trenches" are often quite willing and even eager to share a few stories. In John's case, reaching out to one or two others who have been project leads for opening other stores would be well worth the time. Networking from those project leaders to others they might recommend may be helpful as well.

Another important resource for any project is the authority required to make the decisions needed in a project. Projects, for example, often need the help of others. The authority to acquire their help can work wonders when needed. Authority comes from those higher up in the host organization who will actively champion project work. Their support needs to be acquired early in the planning process and maintained throughout the life of the project.

Costs

Project costs are always of concern to clients, host organizations, and project teams. Although ballpark figures tend to get discussed early on in projects, it is important to understand that early ballpark figures often determine stakeholders' expectations. Those expectations need to be handled carefully right from the beginning.

Outside clients and even those in the host organization can underestimate true project costs. Outside clients, for example, tend to overlook a lot of project activities (e.g., the costs of simply administering a project) and underestimate the actual costs of project items (e.g., not considering Social Security, Medicare, and health benefits, among other personnel costs).[9] Higher-level managers in the host organization can also overlook cost items that are more apparent to project leaders working in the trenches (e.g., supplies, travel, overhead charges, equipment, and materials as well as administrative costs).

All this speaks to the fact that project leaders need to be very careful when dealing with project costs and the expectations of others. In John's case, he might get a reasonable ballpark figure by calling project leaders who have opened stores in the past, getting their final costs, and then adjusting for things like inflation and other items. This is called "top-down" or "analogous" budgeting, because it applies the costs of a similar project to the project at hand. The full costs, however, await "bottom up" budgeting based on an accounting of all project tasks (addressed in the next chapter).

Whether a project leader is asked to develop a project budget (as in John's case) or is given one by the performing organization, he or she needs to think through the implications in terms of deliverables and scheduled delivery very carefully and convey the implications to his or her manager and clients. This is a valuable service but one that often requires, at the same time, both tact and assertiveness.

Timeline

Like costs, the time allocated to get a project done largely determines what *can* be done. Generally speaking, clients and host organizations want projects done as quickly as possible. Project teams, ever pressed for time, generally want more of it.

John's case is a typical one. Ms. Byrnes scheduled a hard completion date of June 15th without initial consultation with the project leader. That time horizon, however, might well affect some deliverables. A direct mail promotion, for example, might take more than 6 weeks to set up using standard operating procedures. Some equipment usually brought in for store openings may well be committed on that weekend by the vendors who supply it. Although more money can often speed things up or change the priorities of vendors, added costs, as we have seen, have issues of their own.

Project leaders need to make stakeholders aware of the implications of time demands just as they do for project costs. Like cost estimations, ballpark, top-down time horizons can be estimated from the times taken to complete similar projects. Nevertheless, each project is unique, and clients need to understand that time as well as costs will affect what deliverables are possible.

Developing and Signing
Off on the Project's Charter

Performing organizations that routinely host outside projects for their business often kick off a project with a project charter. A project charter is based on a good description of a project, and it formally authorizes the project to proceed. The idea of developing and using a project charter is a good one for all project leaders whether or not their organizations require one. A project charter can be as formal as those used in project organizations or as informal as a memo or e-mail that has been approved by the project's sponsor—the manager with the authority to commit organizational resources to a project.

A project charter describes the project in enough detail that a sponsor can make an informed decision about whether to commit resources to it. It describes the mission of a project and ties that mission to the project's main objectives and deliverables. It lays out expected timelines and enough cost information that all stakeholders can make an informed decision to move ahead. A project charter should also address what will be needed to make the project successful. Time and budget needs are based on time and cost estimates. Human and other resources needed are described. What levels of authority are needed to conduct project activities should be considered, as well as any other assumptions critical to project success (e.g., the availability of key personnel).

Just the production of such a charter will force the project leader to consider the important elements of the project at its initiation. The formal acceptance of the charter by key stakeholders, however, signals to the project leader that the project can, indeed, move ahead as planned. It signals, as well, that the project is a legitimate undertaking that has the full backing it needs to achieve its goals. Table 2.2 presents some key questions leaders can use as a check-off list when first developing a project. Although the questions are not exhaustive, they provide a jumping-off point for project leaders as they begin to put projects together for the first time.

Table 2.2   Initiation Check-Off List

There are many issues to consider when first planning a project. Listed here are a few of the more important questions leaders should ask themselves as they move through the project initiation process. The questions are meant to encourage project leaders to think through the issues involved and are meant to be used as a point of departure rather than as a comprehensive listing.

- What is the mission or purpose of the project?

- What are the key project objectives?

- What are the client's final and interim deliverables? Are there any quality requirements? Show extra care in the development of these; they are your "contracted" items.

- What is the basic scope of project work that will need to be done? Consider work to produce the deliverables and any administrative requirements.

- What resources will be required? Consider human resources, material, equipment, facilities, and any other resource that may be needed. Include consideration of subcontracts for outsourcing. Consider any special arrangements that may be needed.

- What is the timeline for the project? Can the project be completed in that time?

- What is the budget for the project? Will it cover the costs required?

- What are the key areas of risk for the project in terms of deliverables, work requirements, costs, and time?

- Who are the key stakeholders of this project? What are their requirements? To what extent can they affect the project? Consider the client, higher management (including your direct supervisor), others on the project team, end users, external vendors, and internal suppliers of project resources. Make sure you have contacted all relevant stakeholders, whether or not they are key players. Make sure you have extended discussions with key players about their expectations.

- Who can you quickly contact to get information about projects similar to this one? Ask about deliverables, work scope, timelines, budget, and special or unforeseen problems that arose that you should consider in your own risk assessments. Ask for referrals to others who have had similar projects whom you can contact.

- Have you developed a written charter of the project? Has it been approved by the key stakeholders of the project? Has it been formally accepted and approved by those in management who have the authority to approve the project and allocate funds and other organizational resources for its budget?

Once the charter is developed and accepted, it can be used as the basis for developing a full project plan. The project plan will nail down project specifics and guide the project through its life cycle. We will be attending to the other elements of the project plan in the next two chapters, but it is appropriate now to specify just what goes into a project plan.

The Project Plan

Before they begin actual construction, contractors need blueprints of the building they are to construct. So, too, do project leaders need their own blueprints of the project—the project plan. Project plans will vary in content, complexity, and detail depending on the projects they address. At the very least, however, a project plan should include a number of common elements.

- **The project's mission statement:** The mission statement lays out the general purpose of the project.

- **The project's objectives:** What the project is trying to achieve in specific terms.

- **All deliverables and quality criteria:** Deliverables include both the final set of deliverables to be given to the client and all interim deliverables. If required, any quality criteria or other specifications for those deliverables should be included.

- **A complete work breakdown structure:** This is a complete specification of all project work that needs to be done—the project's scope. We cover this in Chapter 3.

- **The project schedule:** This is a schedule showing which tasks are to be done by what dates in the project. Typically, the schedule specifies the start and end or completion dates for all project tasks. We cover this in Chapter 4.

- **All resources needed for the project:** These include human resources, materials, equipment, facilities, and the like.[10]

- **The project's budget:** The budget should be laid out by project task so it can be used to control costs throughout the project as those tasks are performed.

- **Risk assessments:** Project risks include those that threaten the attainment of project objectives, push back project dates, increase project costs, or detrimentally affect project deliverables.

As can be seen, the project plan is really a series of project documents. You can think of these documents, for a moment, as all collected together into a three-ring binder.[11] Project leaders will carry this binder wherever they go on a project and continuously refer to it as the project moves forward. They will also keep updating the plan as changes are required. They will add other documents to the plan as well—authorization for changes, sign-offs for work done, and the like. Keeping track of all these documents is an important administrative task for project leaders. They always seem to come in handy down the road.

As we finish this chapter, we see that our project charter has given us a good start at creating our project plan. Its purpose, after all, was to give stakeholders a ballpark idea of the project in enough detail to allow a decision to move forward and make a commitment to the project the leader had envisioned. We turn now to developing the work breakdown structure of the project plan and how it is used to make the more precise estimates leaders need of the resource, cost, and time demands of the project.

Summary

All projects have a mission. That mission is to help address the problems and needs of the project's clients. Mission statements clarify the goals and aims of a project in those terms. As such, they help give general guidance to a project. They help to orient and direct project teams, for example, and anyone else who might work with or contribute to a project. When they are developed in concert with a project's principal stakeholders, mission statements provide a common understanding of the project that can help tie together the often diverse interests of stakeholders. This common ground can be used in bringing together stakeholders to negotiate matters of common concern as needed.

All projects also have a number of stakeholders who have a vested interest in the mission of a project. The client, of course, has a stake in the project solving his or her problem. The organization hosting the project has a stake in seeing the project run smoothly and, if appropriate, making a profit. The project team is a stakeholder, including the project leader. The team members want to see the project become a success, of course, but they would like not to be overstretched and overcommitted in doing so. End users are those who will ultimately use the output of the project. Suppliers are stakeholders, too. External suppliers make money from supplying a project. Internal suppliers, on the other hand, often have to supply resources to projects without compensation, putting a strain on the project/supplier relationship that needs attention. In all cases, stakeholders are people—people who can make decisions that can have an important effect on the project. Project leaders, then, need to be able to work with them successfully.

Once a project's mission has been clarified by its stakeholders, project objectives and deliverables need to be specified. Project objectives are specific goals that must be attained for the mission to be achieved. Deliverables are the products and services that will fulfill those specific goals. Project objectives and deliverables are better when they are SMART: specific, measurable, actionable, realistic, and time limited.

Project objectives and deliverables help the client see the project in concrete terms, and they provide the project team with clear direction. They also help often diverse stakeholders negotiate concrete project outcomes that will satisfy their interests. Certainly, project leaders need to help their stakeholders come to agreement about what specific objectives and deliverables will satisfy them before moving ahead.

Once a project's mission, objectives, and deliverables have clarified its direction, project leaders need to make initial assessments of a project's work requirements, its resource needs, its costs, and its timeline. All projects require resources to get them done, and an initial estimate needs to be made of them. Key among these are human resources—people with the knowledge, skills, and abilities to get the project done. In addition to all the other resources a project needs, two other, often overlooked, resources are information useful for the project and the authority to take the actions needed when conducting the project. A little time invested in attention to these resources can reap large benefits later.

All project stakeholders are interested in project costs—each for their own reasons and concerns. Initial ballpark estimates for projects will be needed, but care must be taken that the expectations of stakeholders are not inflated. Project leaders can often get an initial ballpark estimate by top-down or analogous estimating. To do so, a similar project is selected, its final costs are noted, and then they are modified to fit the specifics of the present project.

Stakeholders are also interested in the amount of time it will take to complete a project. As with cost estimates, a top-down time estimate can be developed from similar projects adjusted for present circumstances. Often both costs and a project's timeline are simply given to a project leader. In these cases, it is best for the leader to clarify the implications of such hard constraints on project deliverables.

Before a proposed project gets fully under way, the leader should develop a project charter. The project charter describes what the project is trying to achieve and how it intends to do so. It includes estimated costs and a project schedule or timeline as well as a description of needed resources. Once a sponsoring manager in the host organization or the leader's client formally sanctions the charter, the project has the agreement of key stakeholders to move forward.

The project charter is the first step in producing a project plan—the blueprint project leaders use to fully understand and run a project. At the very least, a project plan consists of a mission statement and the project's objectives. A complete breakdown of all project work will be needed, along with a schedule of when specific tasks will be done. Resource needs require attention as well as a project budget. Finally, assessments need to be made regarding various risks to the project—threats to deliverables, costs, and time required for the project.

Review Questions

1. Define and characterize mission statements. What roles do mission statements play for a project?

2. What are the elements that characterize the political role of mission statements?

3. What is a stakeholder in a project? Who are the stakeholders reviewed in this chapter, and what are their concerns or interests in a project?

4. What are the objectives and deliverables in a project? How do they differ from one another and from the mission statement? What roles do objectives and deliverables play for a project?

5. What are some of the key resources that need to be considered early in the development of a project?

6. How might ballpark estimates of project costs be developed early in the project? How should cost estimates be handled when working with the project's stakeholders?

7. What is a project charter? What forms can a project charter take? What are reasons that a project charter should be developed and used?

Exercise

1. Work individually or as a team to develop a project charter.
   a. Focus on a project that is relevant to you or your team.
   b. Focus on and define the basic problems the project will address.
   c. Identify the major stakeholders in the project and their interests.
   d. Develop a mission statement for the project and its major objectives. Develop one or more project deliverables for each project objective.
   e. Identify some of the key resources you will need for the project. Be as specific and concrete as possible given the needs of your project.
   f. Estimate the costs and time needed for the project. These estimates are for purposes of writing up the project charter only.

    g. Write up a one- to two-page charter for the project. Frame the charter as a proposal for approval by higher management in your host organization or by your client.

Endnotes

1. The term *performing organization* is the one used by: Project Management Institute. (2000). *Guide to the project management body of knowledge.* Newtown Square, PA: Author. *Host organization* is the label preferred here, however.

2. This "market segment," in fact, accounts for a great deal of the growth in the demand for project leaders.

3. A careful reader might note that the June 15th date set by Carol Byrnes has been changed to "on or about." Project leaders often take such constraints as "given" without question. Although Ms. Byrnes no doubt has this date in mind, further preliminary work may find it unacceptable. For example, some other event might be occurring on that date that would undermine the whole purpose of the opening (e.g., an automotive show attracting business users of the store or a NASCAR event attracting retail customers of the store).

4. In the development of a new product, for example, interim deliverables may include prototypes, testing, and marketing plans as well as the end product itself. Quite often, interim deliverables are required to decide whether to proceed with the project. We will see in the next chapter, as well, that the project can produce deliverables for itself in the form of planning and administrative products and services.

5. A common mistake, in fact, is for managers to simply dictate objectives to project leaders early on without carefully thinking them through. If so, project leaders need to review the given objectives to see their full implications. These need to be brought to the attention of the manager privately and, hopefully, before the manger makes any public declarations of the project's objectives.

6. While the acronym "SMART" is a common one, the "A" has been used to refer to a number of goal criteria. Achievable, accurate, and action oriented are a few of them. I prefer actionable as it is least redundant and focuses attention on making things happen.

7. Using a "single text" procedure is one way of approaching this issue. The project leader lays out an initial listing of objectives and deliverables and lets the stakeholders discuss among themselves how to alter it. As they do so, the project leader facilitates negotiations with what can and cannot be done and addresses the interests of each stakeholder in terms of the project's mission. The stakeholders themselves, then, assume the responsibility for negotiating their own agreement.

8. In project and matrix organizations, sharing personnel among projects is a standard operating procedure. Even here, however, sharing human resources often causes conflict.

9. It should be mentioned that the costs of a project are very different from the price of a project. The costs of a project are borne by the host or performing

organization. The price of a project is what the host organization charges the client and includes other associated overhead costs and profits to be made. Project leaders in host organizations rarely discuss costs with outside clients and are usually not involved in the pricing of a project at all.

10. Unique resources are particularly important to include. If you need a particular person to work on some task because of his or her singular expertise, that should be noted and arranged far in advance. The same goes for any special equipment, materials, and so forth.

11. Actually, project plans are usually kept as computer files with some paper backup.

3

The Work Breakdown Structure

Introduction   38
    The Compliance Project   38
    Chapter Overview   39
The Work Breakdown Structure and Its Project Role   39
    Roles Played by a WBS   41
        Laying Out the Scope of Project Work   42
        Providing the Foundation of All Project Estimates   42
        Helping to Provide the Organizational
          Structure of the Project   52   42
Producing a WBS   43
    Core Tasks   43
    Support Tasks   44
        Project Planning   44
        Project Administration   45
Using the Output of a WBS   46
    Resource, Time, and Cost Estimates   47
        Estimating Resources   48
        Estimating Time Requirements   49
        Estimating Costs   50
    Developing a Project Structure   50
Summary   55
Review Questions   56
Exercise   56

Endnotes	57
Figure 3.1: Illustration of a Work Breakdown Structure for Golden Years Compliance Project	40
Table 3.1: Project Costs: Illustration of One Task Cost Estimate	51
Table 3.2: Work Breakdown Structure Check-Off List	54

Introduction

The Compliance Project

Linda Swain had been recently hired by AgenCorp as director for its elder care center in Portland, Oregon: Golden Years. AgenCorp had been acquiring elder care facilities across the country, and the Portland facility was one of its larger acquisitions with well over a hundred beds. Linda was a registered nurse with a great deal of experience from "floor care" to higher levels of nursing administration in larger facilities like this one. She replaced the last director, who was let go by AgenCorp. In addition to the usual duties of a director, Linda was charged to remedy a number of problems held over from the previous owners, but one was potentially "fatal": threatened decertification by the state of Oregon. In the two previous inspections, Golden Years had received a "no pass" based on a number of violations ranging across all operations of Golden Years. One of Linda's most pressing projects on being hired was to make sure Golden Years passed the state inspection on its next 6-month review.

The mission of Linda's Compliance Project was pretty clear: Golden Years must pass the next state inspection in 6 months. After looking into the matter, Linda was able to put together more specific project objectives as well. State certification addressed each of the five main divisions of AgenCorp's facility: administration, food service/nutrition, physical therapy, medical care, and hospitality services. Passing certifications in these five areas presented themsevles as natural project objectives. The state inspection criteria for each area provided Linda with the detail she would need to make the project objectives and deliverables specific and measurable. In addition, Linda decided that she wanted to establish standard operating procedures (SOPs) for each division to make sure Golden Years would pass state inspections in the future.

The challenge now was to figure out what specific tasks needed to be done to achieve those objectives. Along with identifying the necessary tasks to be done, Linda would need to know who would do them, what resources they would need to get the job done, what everything would cost, and how to organize the project so she could exercise proper command and control of it.

All these rest on developing a work breakdown structure of the project—the focus of this chapter.

Chapter Overview

Projects are unique, one-of-a-kind endeavors. Even when a project leader has determined what to deliver, figuring out how to do it can be overwhelming. The principal approach to use in addressing any large problem is to break it down into smaller ones. The same goes for projects. Linda's first step was to break "Golden Years needs to pass certification" into "Golden Years needs to pass certification in each of its five divisions and develop SOPs for each area to pass in the future"—her project objectives. The task now was to break down those objectives into the larger jobs needed to achieve them and then to lay out the more detailed tasks to get each larger job done. The result of this process is called a *work breakdown structure*, and it forms the foundation of any project. In this chapter, we take a close look at what work breakdown structures are and the roles they play in projects. We then go on to discuss how to construct them and wrap up by addressing some of the ways work breakdown structures are used.

The Work Breakdown Structure and Its Project Role

According to the Project Management Institute, a work breakdown structure (WBS) is "a deliverable-oriented grouping of project elements that organizes and defines the work scope of the project. Each descending level represents an increasingly detailed definition of the project work."[1] Another way of putting this is that a WBS encompasses all those tasks that must be done to complete the project—to produce its deliverables. Those tasks are laid out in a hierarchy of larger jobs to get done, the smaller tasks needed to do those larger jobs, and so on in more and more detail until one gets to the most detailed tasks needed.

Figure 3.1 shows part of what Linda's WBS might look like. The mission of the Compliance Project is to pass state certification in 6 months and to produce SOPs to do so in the future. This mission is broken down into five basic project objectives: Each organizational division is to pass certification and develop its own SOPs—Administration, Physical Therapy, Food and Nutrition, Medical Care, and Hospitality Services (breakdowns for Physical Therapy and Hospitality Services are not shown for reasons of space). You might also note there are breakdowns for Project Planning and Project Administration. These cover project support activities, which we will cover later.

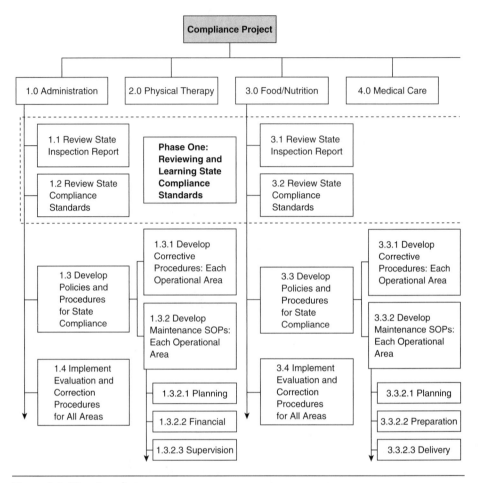

Figure 3.1 *(Continued)*

To pass certification and develop SOPs for the future, Linda has determined that each area will need to review its earlier inspections to target past and possible future problems ("Review State Inspection Report" 1.1, 2.1, 3.1, 4.1, and 5.1). A deliverable for each of these tasks might be a brief report detailing those problems. Another task that Linda believes each area should do is to "Review State Compliance Standards" for its area (1.2, 2.2, 3.2, 4.2, and 5.2). This task might produce a number of deliverables including a briefing report to be given at a meeting of division heads and an initial check-off list to be used later in developing the area's SOPs. Finally, Linda believes both reviews need to be completed before anything else can be done toward certification. Together, then, the tasks will compose Phase One of the Compliance Project. This kind of graphical representation of a

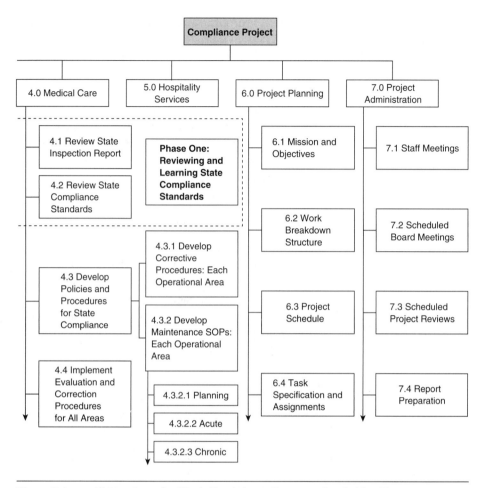

Figure 3.1   Illustration of a Work Breakdown Structure for Golden Years
                Compliance Project

NOTE: SOP = standard operating procedure.

WBS can serve a variety of purposes. We will come back to it throughout
Chapter 3.

Roles Played by a WBS

It is hard to overstate the importance of a WBS for a project. It is the foundation of virtually everything relevant to actually conducting it. Laying out
the scope of project tasks that need to be done, estimating what it will take
to do those tasks, and helping to show how tasks, people, and other project

elements are to be organized into a project structure are some of the more important roles played by a WBS discussed here.

Laying Out the Scope of Project Work

The scope of project work is the sum total of all work that must be done on a project. It does not take long to realize that a project's true scope is probably not completely understood until it is fully broken down into its component tasks. An important goal of a WBS, then, is to make sure that all the tasks necessary to complete a project are identified before the project actually begins.

Providing the Foundation of All Project Estimates

Only after a project has been broken down to the detail of project tasks can a project leader get a precise, bottom-up estimate of what it will take to complete the project. These include any resource requirements, the time it is likely to take to do the project, the costs of each task, and assessments of risk—the chances of getting the task done on time and on budget. Although a project leader might have a good guess about what it may take to complete a particular project component, he or she will not have a precise estimate until it is based on a WBS.

Helping to Provide the Organizational Structure of the Project

Once a project is broken down into its tasks, it can be "put back together" again into a project structure. The Compliance Project shown in Figure 3.1 probably reminds you of an organizational chart.[2] That is no coincidence. Managers and project leaders both go through the same kind of "means-ends" analysis to put their organizations and projects together. What they are trying to accomplish—their goals—are the ends they want to achieve. Next, they need to find the means to achieve them. In the case of a project, the project's mission is its ultimate end—its ultimate goal. Project objectives are the means to achieve it. Next, the project objectives themselves play the role of ends and they, in turn, need to be broken down into the basic jobs—the means—to achieve them. Those jobs are generally large and made up of many smaller tasks. They will need to be broken down, then, into smaller and smaller jobs until it is pretty clear what exactly needs to be done. The end result is a collection of project tasks or "work packages" that define the most detailed work scope of the project.

Going back to the Compliance Project in Figure 3.1, the ultimate end is passing state certification and developing SOPs to do so in the future. Each division passing certification and developing its own SOPs are the means to achieve that end. Each area passing its own certification now becomes an end in itself, and other tasks become the means to achieve it. And so it goes until the WBS is complete and the tasks are ready to be arranged into a project structure.

In summary, a WBS is a comprehensive listing of all project work. Once a project is broken down into its component tasks, leaders are better able to assess the true scope of work needed to get it done. They are also better able to assess its resource, time, and cost requirements. Another important outcome of a WBS is a project structure that will facilitate the kinds of resource allocation, staffing and delegation, and related command and control needs of a project. The project structure is created by reassembling the tasks broken down in a WBS in a way that helps the allocation of project work and the command and control of the project.

Producing a WBS

The technical name for breaking down jobs into ever-smaller tasks is "decomposition." Larger jobs are de-composed into all the tasks needed to complete the job. This is usually done step by step with progressively more and more detail. The point at which leaders stop is when they believe they have enough task detail to reasonably estimate things like personnel and other resource needs, the true costs of the task, and the risks associated with getting that particular task done.[3]

Although this can be a very straightforward process, it is often fraught with error. Chief among them is to forget some task or set of tasks that needs to be done to complete the project or some of its components. Being people after all, project leaders can overlook things, and they have their blind spots too. It is a good idea, then, for project leaders to bring in other experts to review the tasks that need to be done. If these experts can include key members of the project, leaders get a double benefit: expert advice and an early start at organizing and orienting the important members of the project team itself.

When developing a WBS, project leaders have a natural tendency to focus on the core tasks of the project. Often overlooked, however, are the necessary support tasks to pull off a project on time and on budget.

Core Tasks

Core tasks are all those tasks necessary to produce the products and services that will be delivered to the client. These tend to command the most project attention because clients and the host organization are most concerned abut them. Despite the attention they command, many core tasks are overlooked when producing a WBS. People tend to think of those tasks most directly related to producing a good or a service, for example, but tend to overlook logistical or preparatory work for those tasks. In Linda's case, the top staff will need copies of the state's compliance policies and, likely, more user-friendly reviews of them. Linda may even need to provide training for herself and her top staff to fully understand state policies, criteria, and inspection procedures. Securing those reviews and providing that training can be easily overlooked as important considerations in breaking the project's work down.

When breaking down core activities, then, it pays to move through the tasks in a deliberate way, thinking of all the related activities needed to achieve the higher-level goal. Reaching out to others can be a real benefit to leaders in this endeavor. Those who have conducted similar projects or project components can provide valuable information. Those who will actually do the project work can be of help too. When they focus their attention on what the task needs to get it done, their operational experience can help flesh out the work breakdown so the project leader will not overlook important and necessary tasks.

Support Tasks

Support tasks are all those tasks necessary for conducting the project itself. They are the most overlooked components of project work, and they need to be included in every WBS for at least two reasons. First, like any task, they consume time and resources. Somebody *will* pay for them; the only question is who. The client is unlikely to pay for unplanned expenses, and your host organization will be far from happy to do so. That leaves the project leader and project team to pay—most often with uncompensated overtime! Second, support work needs to be done so the project runs smoothly. Without proper support, work on the core components of a project will suffer. Two basic kinds of support activities are project planning and project administration.

Project Planning

Project planning is really the first phase of any project, and it involves all those tasks that we are addressing in the first section of this book and more. Quite often, project planning is viewed as a kind of overhead. Basic planning needs to be done before a project is approved, and developing a more detailed project plan is needed before actually running the project. Clients are often reluctant to pay for a project plan that may not suit their needs. Project planning takes time, however, and it consumes resources and costs money. When project leaders are asked to lay out plans for a project, they need to be aware that they will be consuming a fair amount of resources to do so. They need strategies, then, not to carry the effort too far without reimbursement or increased possibilities that the project will, in fact, go forward.

One basic strategy is to plan incrementally. Once a mission statement has been developed, project objectives laid out, and a best-guess estimate made of costs and time for the project, it is time to pause and reflect whether the project is worth moving forward as it was initially conceived. Performing organizations that routinely conduct project work generally have SOPs to do just this sort of thing. Projects go through an initiating process of initial planning that results in a project charter as discussed in Chapter 2. Key stakeholders use the initial plan of the charter to decide whether to OK further work on the project and then keep track as the planning moves forward. The whole idea is to decide whether a project is worth the effort early in the project cycle rather than later on when too many resources have already been expended.

This process can be followed in other, less "project formal" situations as well. When handed a project by one's boss, for example, quick preliminary estimates of work scope, costs, time estimates, and likely benefits should be shared with him or her as soon as possible. As another example, if a consultant is working with a client on a new project, the consultant might include an initial charge for project planning to some agreed level of detail. Once those plans are developed, the project reaches a decision point at which both the client and the consultant as project leader decide whether to move forward. If so, the initial planning charge can be rolled into the overall project cost structure. The important point here is to keep the key stakeholders informed about the project costs from the very beginning, get them on board, and "track" them through the planning process until they literally—as well as psychologically—buy into it.

Project Administration

Another support process often overlooked is project administration. Even small projects can generate a number of administrative tasks, and those tasks seem to increase geometrically as project size increases. Quite a few administrative tasks are associated with complying with the rules and regulations of the host organization. Leaders, for example, are often required to keep track of and report on their project's costs and budget expenditures. Other administrative tasks are required for project communications. Project meetings with staff, clients, and others, for example, can take a great deal of project work and consume a great deal of personnel time. Command and control activities also require time and resource expenditures. Most projects have milestones included in their schedules to indicate when certain tasks are to be done. Although milestones are defined as "no resource use" events, preparing for them usually consumes quite a bit of resources in conducting compliance checks and corrections, developing reports, and meeting with clients or project leaders. Formally including support activities in the project's WBS, then, is necessary.

In summary, producing the project's WBS defines the scope of project work in real, concrete terms. Quite often, however, tasks are overlooked, even critical ones. Part of the reason is time. Project leaders are pressured to begin project work before the project itself is fully laid out. Another reason is technical. Because a project is a unique, one-of-a-kind endeavor, all the necessary tasks to get it done have not yet been developed. Still a third reason is human. Project leaders have their own blind spots and can become impatient. We tend to overlook things we take for granted when we want to move on with our projects. Project leaders need to remember, however, that they and their project teams are likely to bear most of the cost of overlooked work. That fact alone should encourage leaders to reflect a little longer and reach out to others to make sure the WBS is complete. Those others include experts in the technical areas of project work, those who have had experience in similar project work, and those who will be actually working on the project producing the deliverables envisioned.

The Compliance Project is a case in point. Linda Swain might well consider bringing in an outside consultant with expertise in certification during the initial planning stages as well as later in the project. She might also consider taking her counterpart at another elder care center out to lunch to chat about the project, particularly if her counterpart has had similar experiences with certification. Finally, Linda would do well to discuss her plans with her second-in-commands to better assess the tasks that likely lie ahead as well as bring them on board early in the planning process. A few hours invested in these kinds of consultation activities early in the project will likely save Linda endless problems further down the road.

Using the Output of a WBS

One of the very nice things about constructing a WBS is that it focuses a project leader's attention in useful ways. First, attention is focused on the broader project and its major objectives and deliverables. Next, attention is focused on the major jobs that must be done to produce each deliverable. This process continues until attention is finally focused on the actual work tasks or work packages themselves.

Once the work packages are broken out, the project leader can better estimate what it will take to get the project done. The leader can also begin the task of reassembling those tasks into a coherent project structure he or she can use as part of the project plan to lead the project itself. We will look first at the kinds of estimates project leaders make using their WBS to guide them. We conclude by examining how the tasks in a WBS can be used to create a project structure suitable for work allocation and command and control.

Resource, Time, and Cost Estimates

There are two basic ways of developing estimates in projects: top-down or analogous estimating and bottom-up estimating. Analogous estimating looks at actual resource, time, and cost estimates of similar projects or project components. These estimates are used as a base, and adjustments are made to reflect the conditions of the present project. There are two primary benefits to this approach. One is that estimates can be made fairly quickly if records have been kept of previous project work. Another advantage is that this technique benefits from hindsight. Estimating resources, time, or costs can overlook any number of things before tasks are actually done. Once the tasks are completed, however, everything that was overlooked has made itself known. The principal drawback is that previous projects reflect previous conditions and needs. The present project, even if similar, is nevertheless unique and can differ in substantial ways that will be overlooked unless more detailed estimating is used. This problem is made worse when estimates rely more on memory than on records and consideration of current project differences are not given the care they deserve.

Bottom-up estimating looks at each task itself and estimates the resources, time, and cost to do it from a "zero base." For each task in the WBS, for example, the costs of human resources, equipment, material, and other charges are calculated and rolled up for the entire project. The principal advantage of this approach is precision. When all tasks and task elements have been identified, more precise estimates can be made. Still another advantage is that bottom-up estimating focuses the leader's attention on the costs of each work package. This comes in handy later when making sure project work is moving ahead according to budget. A principal drawback is that this approach takes a fair amount of time and resources itself. Another drawback is that, quite often, task elements and even entire tasks are overlooked in developing a WBS that then affects the precision that bottom-up estimating promises.

It is likely best to combine the two approaches when estimating resource, time, and cost elements of any project. Bottom-up estimating brings potential precision and top-down or analogous estimating brings past experience to the whole process. In any event, estimating project needs is itself a project activity that consumes resources, takes time, and costs money. At some point, a tradeoff must be made between ever-elusive precision and good-enough estimates to move forward. When estimating resource, time, and cost requirements, however, project leaders should keep a few things in mind.

Estimating Resources

Resource estimates generally focus on the human resources, equipment, and materials needed to do the job. Human resource assessments tend to focus on the project team members because they usually are the ones doing most of the work. The knowledge, skills, and abilities needed to produce the task's deliverables should be considered as well as the number of personnel needed to finish on time. These estimates are then used for later personnel decisions, cost estimates, and scheduling.

Outside personnel needed to complete a job should also be considered. Those who charge the project tend to get the most attention for obvious reasons. Linda, for example, plans to have trainers and consultants help in the Compliance Project. Often, however, host organizations volunteer their own people to help the project in some way or another. Even if the organization does not care to charge the project for these personnel, you can bet the people involved and their supervisors care—they care in terms of time taken off their work to do the project's. The number of hours needed from them, then, requires careful thought with due consideration given to their other duties. Other kinds of outside human resources also need to be considered. Outside regulators, for example, are often needed to certify the quality of work or the quality of the work environment. Projects may or may not bear the actual costs of such reviews. Even if they do not, it is best to include them in the WBS as a no-cost activity to keep track of them for later scheduling.

Finally, the contributions of one important project member are often overlooked—the project leader. The project leader needs to assess the extent to which he or she will be needed in any particular task. We will address delegation in another chapter, and project leaders should not have to closely supervise every task. Nevertheless, project leaders have a number of tasks that they lead (e.g., planning, conducting project meetings, and performing budget reviews) and a number of quality control, command, and other responsibilities that will require their attention (e.g., at various milestones in the project, at times of negotiations, hiring and training, meeting with clients, and communicating with outside stakeholders). Project leaders need to consider their own time, then, as a limited resource that needs careful allocation.

Establishing resource estimates for equipment and materials also requires attention. Any special equipment needed to do the task must be considered, as well as any materials needed. The importance of getting the right tools and materials to the right workers at the right time is often underappreciated. The logistics behind this task are often complex, however, and will play an important role in finishing a project on time and on budget.

Finally, other needed resources are often overlooked or simply assumed. Office space, office equipment, and supplies, for example, are often overlooked in planning. In many cases, they are made available by the host organization. If the project is occurring offsite, however, resources like these cannot be assumed. Not to be forgotten are intangible resources like information and authority. Information is always a prized resource in projects because they are each unique. Linda, for example, is willing to pay a great deal of money for information about certification (i.e., the trainers) and information about the extent to which her project will actually meet state standards (i.e., with an initial, "shakedown" review by an outside consultant). As a project leader walks through the tasks of a project, information needs should be considered as well. So, too, should the requisite authority to do a project task. Often, project tasks must be done in organizational arenas outside of the scope of a lead person's authority. Although Linda does not need to worry too much about the scope of her authority for this project, those who report to her may have to. The project duties they perform may well take them beyond their normal areas of authority, and they will need higher level authority to do so.

Estimating Time Requirements

Time demands are often given at the project level. Linda has 6 months, for example, to meet state certification standards. Clients usually have an idea about when they would like to see a project completed. Estimating the time requirements for individual project tasks is the first step in arranging those tasks to complete the project on time.

Given a certain level of human and other resources, project leaders can estimate how long project tasks will take. Information from similar tasks, set standards, input from the team itself, and the leader's own experience are all inputs to this estimate. In addition to this best guess, the leader may wish to provide pessimistic and optimistic estimates to create an interval of time within which the leader is 95% sure the task will be completed. Pessimistic and optimistic estimates are, in fact, used in Project Evaluation and Review Technique (PERT) scheduling to help adjust for the "time risk" of projects (see Chapter 4). Even if the leader does not use PERT, it is a good idea to estimate a time range for task completion.

This is a good time, too, to consider lag times for a task. Lag time is the amount of time a task needs to "rest" after work has been done on it. For example, once concrete has been poured, smoothed, and finished, it must be left for some time to cure. The job is not really done until the curing time has passed. When thinking through the tasks of a project, then, this kind of required downtime needs to be considered. Some tasks may require advance time as well. For example, a vendor may require advance notification that material is needed before it can be delivered, or an inspector may require a 30-day notice to schedule her inspection visit.

Estimating Costs

For each detailed task in the WBS, the costs of human resources, equipment, materials, and other charges are calculated and rolled up for the project. Care must be taken, however, to include all cost items. Often overlooked costs include travel, long-distance communications, fees charged by regulatory agencies or vendors, inflation adjustments (for multiyear projects), organizational overhead charges, and the like. Table 3.1 gives an example of a spreadsheet layout detailing some costs for one element of the Compliance Project—consultant reviews of Linda's operations and a feedback report. Similar spreadsheets can be used by project leaders to detail their costs once the project's work has been broken down.

All cost estimates have risk associated with them. One of the most important risks facing the project team is the danger of underestimating the actual costs of the project. In that case, the project team or host organization will have to bear the costs of project completion. It is quite common, then, to add a risk adjustment to the calculated costs for each task that helps to offset that risk. Overestimating project costs also presents a risk: the client going somewhere else to do business. Clients often press project leaders to keep costs down while pressing for product quality in the shortest possible time. A careful cost analysis can help leaders clarify project costs to their clients so that they can appreciate what it takes to produce quality work.

Developing a Project Structure

Once project tasks are broken out into a WBS, they can be reassembled into a project structure. One important use of this structure is that it lets everyone know how they and their work fit into the project and how others depend on them. Another important use is for command and control of the project.

Figure 3.1 shows the Compliance Project's WBS in the form of an organizational chart. Although the figure looks like a traditional organizational chart, a project is really a process composed of many subprocesses. A

Table 3.1 Project Costs: Illustration of One Task Cost Estimate

7.6: Consultant Review of Operations and Feedback Report				
Resource	Quantity	Usage	Cost per Unit	Total Item Cost
Personnel				
Director	1	1 day	$250.00/day	$250.00
Head nurse	4	1 day	150.00/day	600.00
Support nurse	8	2 days	100.00/day	1,600.00
Support staff	4	1 day	60.00	240.00
Equipment				
Computers	8	2 days	00.00	00.00
Materials				
Standard operating procedure manuals each area	5	25 manuals	00.00	00.00
Other (specify)				
Consultants	2	2 days	1,000.00	4,000.00
Travel	2	1 round trip each	1,000.00	2,000.00
Lodging	2	2 days	125.00	500.00
Report	1		500.00	500.00
Overhead charges	Included			
Total resource costs				$9,690.00

process is series of steps that result in some outcome such as a deliverable. Project processes typically cluster into project phases. Projects, for example, have a beginning phase in which planning takes place and resources are gathered, a middle phase in which those resources are used to produce products and services, and an ending phase in which those products and services are delivered to the client and the project is closed down. Quite often, these three project phases can be broken down into several of their own subphases. Linda's project, for example, has an early educational phase in which each organizational area learns about the certification policies and procedures relevant to it. This leads to a policies and procedures development phase in which each area develops the policies and procedures it will use to comply with state requirements generally and prepare for certification visits in particular, and so it goes. Project schedules help make these phases much more apparent and are covered in the next chapter.

The process character of projects also affects how tasks are best grouped together vertically through time. Because process tasks build on one another, it is generally best to use the same human resources throughout the process and, if appropriate, from one phase to another. By doing so, the project takes advantage of the learning curve that accompanies every project task. Those working on later tasks in a project build on their work earlier in the project. For example, within 4.0 Medical Care, we see that SOPs (4.3.2) must be developed for three subareas including Planning (4.3.2.1), Acute Care (4.3.2.2), and Chronic Care (4.3.2.3). It may well be that the same one or two project members should work on all three tasks to take advantage of learning as they develop SOPs in each one of them. Later in the project, these same members are likely to be well suited to play important roles in implementing those SOPs as well.

The process integration of work along with how the work is broken down also affects proper assignment of leadership positions in the project: who are made project leads over parts of the project and what their responsibilities and authority cover. The project leader is responsible for the entire project and has authority over it.[4] Authority may then be delegated to project leads who have authority and direct control over the production and delivery of various project outputs for their components of the project. In Linda's Compliance Project, for example, the division heads of each organizational division may well be considered for these project lead roles whereas Linda would likely assume direct control over project planning and project administration activities as well as her own organizational area of Administration (1.0). Higher-level project leads may, in turn, assign their own project leads to do jobs they need to accomplish their objectives. As authority is delegated down, those higher in the WBS chain have authority over—and are accountable for—work done lower in the WBS chain. Taking a process view of the project, those leading higher-level phases or processes have authority over—and are accountable for—work done in lower-level subprocesses. This approach to grouping project work and project leadership helps achieve both unity of effort and unity of command.[5]

While breaking down and reassembling the WBS, project leaders need also to specify, break out, and assign project work to facilitate command and control. Project tasks or work packages should be broken down in such a way that a concrete deliverable (i.e., a product or service) is produced by it. As was discussed in the last chapter, the best task deliverables are SMART: specific, measurable, actionable, realistic, and time limited. As mentioned previously, the deliverable should be an outcome of a complete phase, process, or subprocess so that those responsible for its output have control over all relevant developmental parts. Although more than one person may be working on a particular project component, to achieve unity of command in the project structure, only one will be the project lead—the one accountable for getting the deliverable produced.[6] Finally, the time allowed for the delivery of task product needs careful consideration. It may well be, for example, that it will take a month or more for a task deliverable to be produced. That timeline, however, can undermine command and control in more complex and larger projects. There is a tendency to put off or "back load" project work when it is given longer lead times. While back loading may well be due to simple procrastination, it is more often due to other competing demands for a team member's attention. We tend to respond to the greatest threat, and those threats tend to be work due tomorrow. Rather than wait for (and hope for) a final product far down the line, it is generally best to break down that work to require concrete products in the interim that will combine to the ultimate deliverable needed. For example, rather than wait a month to receive SOPs for a manager's entire division of four departments, Linda might ask her managers to produce an SOP for each unit, each week. If more time is needed to produce each SOP, Linda might require interim reports and products (outlines, check-off sheets, etc.) to make sure the task is moving as expected. The trade-off to consider here is to make sure product is being produced while not over-supervising or micromanaging good staff.

To conclude, when a project leader has developed the WBS, he or she has taken a giant step forward toward developing an overall project plan. The WBS allows for the development of resource and cost estimates and estimates of how long each task will take. Arranging those tasks through the project's life cycle is the next big step to take. We turn to that task in the next chapter on project scheduling. Table 3.2 presents a list of questions project leaders can ask themselves as they move through the process of creating a WBS and the estimates of work that follows from it. Although not exhaustive, it can provide a check-off list of some key things to consider.

Table 3.2   Work Breakdown Structure Check-Off List

Developing a WBS can be an involved process, not to mention developing the estimates of the resources, costs, and time requirements that flow from it. Listed here are a few key questions leaders should ask themselves as they move through the process of breaking down project work and developing estimates from the breakdown. The questions are meant to encourage project leaders to think through the issues involved and are to be used as a point of departure rather than as a comprehensive listing.

• What are the major jobs that need to be done to complete the core deliverables of this project? What are the tasks that need to be done to finish those major jobs?

• What are the major jobs that need to be done to support the project? Are more planning tasks required? What administrative tasks will be needed? Consider project meetings with the team, clients, and others; interim reports; administrative requirements of the host organization; periodic project reviews; procedures for compliance and certification requirements; and the like.

• Have the project tasks been detailed enough for good estimates to be made about resource, cost, and time requirements?

• Have all outsourced jobs been accounted for? What contracting requirements are needed to ensure deliverables according to specification, on time, and on budget? Will special attention, time, and payments be needed from the team or project leader to ensure delivery? Have these been included in the WBS?

• What are the resource needs for each task in the WBS? Are there any special resources that need to be nailed down or contracted? Are there resources that will be delivered from internal suppliers? What activities or tasks need to be done to ensure delivery? Consider integrating these into your WBS.

• What are the time requirements for each task? Consider whether you should require interim deliverables if the task time horizon for a task completion is too long.

• What are the cost requirements for each task? Have these been figured into a project budget?

• How will the project be organized? Consider grouping project tasks according to work process flow. Who will lead and be assigned to the various tasks and requirements in the WBS? Consider task assignments along work process lines. Assign one and only one person to be accountable for task deliverables and process output.

• Who should review the WBS? Consider future senior team members who will be working on the project tasks. Consider project leaders who have led similar projects. Consider experts in the tasks or fields of work both external and internal to the organization. Consult your supervisor.

Summary

The WBS is the foundation for any project. It defines the scope of work that must be done to produce the deliverables and is the basis for developing bottom-up estimates of the resources, time, and budget needed for the project. It is the foundation, too, on which the project structure is built to facilitate command and control of the project.

Creating a WBS begins by focusing on the deliverables that satisfy the project's objectives and identifying the general jobs needed to achieve them. Those jobs, in turn, become the goals to be reached by more specific tasks. This process of de-composition is followed until the full scope of project work is identified and sufficient detail is reached to actually produce the resource, time, and cost estimates needed for the project.

WBSs are composed of both core and support components. Core components are all those tasks necessary to produce the deliverables promised to a client, and they generally receive the most attention. Support tasks are those activities necessary to see the project through and are often neglected in a WBS. Two main support jobs are project planning and project administration. Because planning is done before core work on a project, it is often neglected as a cost item. When dealing with a client, however, planning can be done in phases of more and more detail with decision points appropriately scheduled. Administrative support includes activities like meetings, client and organizational reports, project reviews, and compliance checks. The fact that they are often seen as incidental to core project activities means they are often overlooked. Whether overlooked or not, however, someone will pay for them.

After the project has been broken down, estimates can be developed and the tasks can be reassembled into a project structure. Project estimates generally focus on resources (human, equipment, and materials), time, and costs. Estimates are most often made by using actual costs of similar or analogous projects as a beginning base or by calculating itemized estimates from each project task from the bottom up. All such estimates are inherently risky, and adjustments need to be developed to help offset those risks.

The project structure is built on the foundation of the WBS. It is built by reassembling its tasks into a structure that facilitates a common, detailed understanding of project work on one hand, and command and control of the project on the other. Because projects are processes, project work is best grouped together into those processes that yield identifiable products and services for the project. Project phases, basic processes within them, and subprocesses within those are grouped together so those working within them can develop an identifiable product or service from beginning to end. To facilitate command and control, leadership in the project should be structured to promote unity of command. In addition, the outputs of project tasks and subprocesses should be defined in SMART and concrete terms. Finally, not too much time should pass before a task or set of tasks produces an identifiable product for possible project review, even if that product is an interim piece of the eventual product or service to be produced.

Review Questions

1. What is a WBS?
   a. What are core and support tasks in a WBS?
   b. Identify two important kinds of support tasks in any project. Why is it important to include them in a WBS?

2. Describe the roles played by a WBS in a project.

3. How is a WBS produced?

4. WBSs are used for a variety of project tasks. One is estimating project resource needs, time, and costs.
   a. What are the two basic ways of estimating resources, time, and costs?
   b. What are their relative advantages and disadvantages?

5. What are the basic resources that need to be estimated in a project?
   a. What are the important considerations for each?

6. What are the important considerations when estimating time requirements of the tasks in a WBS?

7. What are the important considerations when estimating costs in a project?

8. How is a WBS useful in developing the organizational structure of a project?
   a. Cover such issues as how work should be grouped together, the delegation of work to facilitate command and control within broad areas of the project, and the specification of task output to facilitate command and control over the task.

Exercise[7]

1. Work individually or as a team to develop a WBS.
   a. Focus on a project that is relevant to you or your team.
   b. Identify two or three major project deliverables to be produced or services to be delivered.

   c. Develop WBSs for each of these deliverables. Keep breaking down the work into more and more detailed tasks until you are satisfied you can estimate the resource and time needs for them.

   d. Identify the resources needed to accomplish the tasks you have specified.

   e. Estimate the time needs and cost requirements of a significant portion of the tasks you have identified in your WBS.

   f. Arrange the tasks of your WBS into an organizational structure for your project.

   g. Make sure the organizational structure facilitates the delegation of authority in the project. Keep in mind and include any organizational considerations due to project phases.

Endnotes

1. Project Management Institute. (2000). *A guide to the project management body of knowledge.* Newtown Square, PA: Author.

2. Although a traditional organizational structure is pictured in Figure 3.1, many project structures are different from a traditional structure.

3. You probably noticed that every task in the WBS in Figure 3.1 has a number attached to it, and I refer to them often. Although such numbering is optional, it is so important that it should be mandatory. You can think of these numbers in a way similar to those used when writing an outline. Instead of using Roman numerals for headings (e.g., I, I a., II, II a., II a.1), we use a decimal system (e.g., 1.0, 1.1, 2.0, 2.1, 2.2.1).

When this numbering system is applied to a WBS, it coincides with the breakdown logic used to produce the WBS. Higher-level jobs composed of many tasks have higher-level numbers. The tasks that need to be done for those jobs are numbered accordingly as the work is broken down into smaller and smaller tasks. In Linda's WBS, the project objective of administrative operations passing inspection (Administration) is given the highest-level number—a 1.0. This, along with the other most basic project objectives (Physical Therapy, Food/Nutrition, and so on), represents the first major division of the project, and they are all given the highest-level numbers (e.g., 2.0, 3.0) As work is broken down in each of these areas, they are numbered accordingly—1.1, 1.2, and 1.3 for the next level of detail in 1.0 Administration, for example, 1.3.1, 1.3.2, and 1.3.3 for the level of detail after that, and so on.

Such a numbering system is quite useful in keeping track of everything in a project. First, we know which tasks belong to which project task chain. Anything starting with a 3, for example, belongs to the Food/Nutrition component of the project. Second, when personnel decisions are made, project workers assigned to one level of project work (e.g., 3.2.2) are often responsible for all project tasks at levels lower than that number (e.g., 3.2.2.1 to 3.2.2.9). Third, project management software makes use of this numbering system in a variety of processing routines. Fourth, people reviewing the project can find components of the project more easily when looking for heading numbers than heading titles alone. Finally, when reporting on a project, heading numbers can be used to establish parallels between project components and project tasks.

4. In matrix and project organizations, there is often an intentional violation of unity of command, and a project leader's authority over a project can be shared with others who may have authority over some personnel or activities.

5. Unity of effort ensures that the work product fits with other products to produce project deliverables efficiently and effectively. Unity of command means that project members have only one immediate supervisor, and there is only one supervisor accountable for work under his or her purview. In addition, those supervisors are arranged in a coherent hierarchy of authority from the lowest to the highest levels. Project and matrix organizations interfere with unity of command in projects, with project staff reporting to both the project leader or manager and another organizational manager (e.g., a department head or functional manager). Project leaders need to manage this inherent conflict of command and not make it worse in the project itself.

6. An old management saying goes, "When more than one person is responsible for getting work done, no one is responsible for getting work done."

7. If you have project management software, use it to do these tasks.

4

Project Scheduling

Introduction	60
The Bio-Informatics Project	60
Chapter Overview	61
Project Schedules: Types and Components	61
Types of Project Schedules	61
The Gantt or Bar Chart	61
The Critical Path Method (CPM)	62
The Program Evaluation and Review	
Technique (PERT)	63
Components of Project Schedules	63
Activities or Project Tasks	66
Dependencies	66
Lag and Lead Times	67
Milestones	67
The Project Network	68
The Critical Path	68
Slack or Float	68
How to Develop a Project Schedule: Focus—Gantt Charts	69
Break Down Project and Create an Outline of Tasks	69
Review Time Estimates	69
Determine Dependencies	69
Construct the Network of Project Activities	70
Determine the Critical Path	70

Using the Output of a Project Schedule   71
    Visualizing the Project as a Whole   71
        Project Phases   72
        Project Dependencies   72
        Communication to Stakeholders   72
    Revision of Planning Assumptions and Estimates for
      the Project Plan   73
    Making Adjustments to the Plan Throughout the Project   74
    Command and Control   75
Summary   77
Review Questions   78
Exercise   79
Endnotes   79
Figure 4.1 A Simple Bar Chart—Ordering Supplies
    in the Bio-Informatics Project   63
Figure 4.2 A Gantt Chart Illustrating Dr. Howard's
    Bio-Informatics Project   64
Figure 4.3 A Simple Project Network Diagram—
    Dr. Howard's Study   66
Table 4.1: Schedule Check-Off List   76

Introduction

The Bio-Informatics Project

"Be careful what you wish for." That saying kept running through Dr. Dan Howard's head as he looked at the project ahead of him. Dr. Howard, a professor at a large Eastern university, was awarded a $5,000,000 five-year contract by the National Institutes of Health (NIH) to expand his award-winning work in bio-informatics. But it wasn't the bio-informatics research that bothered him now. It was just setting up to do the work! In his proposal to NIH, he allocated time and money to refurbish and convert a large facility at the university's research park into a fully functioning laboratory. Extensive modifications needed to be made on the structure itself, of course, but that was only the beginning. Equipment had to be purchased, delivered, set up, and tested. Supplies needed to be ordered and stored—some of them in special kinds of storage, and some with only a short shelf life. Special security had to be arranged as well—given the nature of his work—and the federal government would review security arrangements to make sure it was up to standard. He also had to hire and train a large contingent of administrative and laboratory staff to support the work of the lead scientists. And he had to do all this and more in just 4 months!

Chapter Overview

Although Dr. Howard's project might be in the category of "high science," the headache he is facing is a common one—how to arrange a lot of different jobs to come together smoothly through time. This chapter addresses that basic issue—how to schedule the work in a project so that things come together like they should to produce whatever is needed at the right time. We begin by looking at different kinds of project schedules and the components that make them up. Next we discuss how schedules are constructed, focusing on the construction of Gantt or bar charts. Finally, we explore some of the ways that project leaders use their schedules.

Project Schedules: Types and Components

The project schedule is the principal tool project leaders use to keep track of a project: whether things are getting done on time, costs are being incurred according to budget, and resources are being used appropriately, as well as what tasks are coming up that need attention and the like. At its heart, a project schedule is simply a list of when project tasks are to begin and end. Because some tasks must finish before other tasks can start, most project schedules tie these tasks together with "dependencies"—linkages that show how tasks are dependent on one another. As projects grow in complexity, their activities and dependencies grow into more and more detailed networks. As you can guess, all of this can get very complicated very quickly. As a result, a number of visual, mathematical, and computer tools have been developed that help project leaders organize and visualize the way project tasks must occur through time.

Types of Project Schedules

Three of the most common scheduling techniques are the Gantt or bar chart, the Critical Path Method, and the Program Evaluation and Review Technique.[1]

The Gantt or Bar Chart

If you count nonprofessionals, Gantt or bar charts are likely the most commonly used scheduling tool because they are fairly easy to learn and can be used in even quite complex projects. Gantt charts illustrate project tasks as bars and place them across the days of a calendar. The length of the bar represents how long the activity will take. The beginning of the bar is placed on the calendar date where the task should begin and the end of the bar shows when the task should end. If a succeeding task (e.g., staff training) cannot begin until a preceding task ends (e.g., staff hiring), the beginning of the succeeding bar is placed at the end of the preceding bar. Sometimes, Gantt charts show arrows between these bars to illustrate their dependency.

Figure 4.1 presents a simple Gantt chart for ordering supplies in the Bio-Informatics Project.[2] The arrows show the dependencies between these tasks, but many Gantt charts leave them out. Figure 4.2 shows how Gantt charts can handle even more complex projects like the Bio-Informatics Project facing Dr. Howard. We will come back to this Gantt chart several more times to illustrate a number of points in this chapter.

Gantt charts are very good tools to use when trying to visualize a project's tasks through time and communicate that information to the project team and others. They are fairly easy to learn and, with modern project management software, can be used to help plan and control quite complex projects.

The Critical Path Method (CPM)

A schedule of tasks can also be shown as a network of arrows and nodes. The arrows show task dependencies, and the nodes show where tasks intersect. Figure 4.3 shows a simple network diagram laying out a study Dr. Howard might conduct in his laboratory once it is set up. In this procedure, Dr. Howard has to spend some time setting up the study he will run. He then needs to do three experiments to compare with one another, each of which has two stages. Finally, he has to analyze the data he developed from them and write up the results in a project report. In the diagram shown in Figure 4.3, the study tasks for activities are represented as nodes with information in them (i.e., the number of the activity, the task name, and time needed to complete it). The arrows simply show the relationship between those activities.[3]

The CPM uses the time estimates for each task to develop the project's critical path, as shown by the double-line arrows in Figure 4.3. A project's

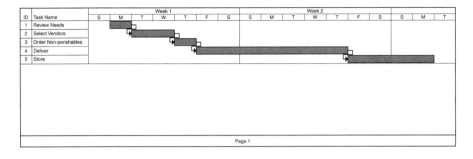

Figure 4.1   A Simple Bar Chart—Ordering Supplies in the Bio-Informatics Project

NOTE: Figure 4.1 was generated using Microsoft Project® 2000.

critical path is that sequence of tasks that, together, will take longer than any other set of tasks to get the project done. Because the project cannot be done any earlier, the critical path determines the earliest end date for the project. Needless to say, this path will command a great deal of the project leader's attention, and we will return to it later. The CPM was created by the DuPont Corporation to aid in their chemical plant projects and has been shown to be very useful across a variety of complex projects.

The Program Evaluation and Review Technique (PERT)

PERT is similar to the CPM but uses three different time estimates for each activity instead of just one: an optimistic time, a likely time, and a pessimistic time for its completion. Each activity, then, has a probability distribution attached to its time estimate. Mathematical techniques like Monte Carlo simulations[4] can be used throughout the project to calculate the probabilities that the project as a whole—or subcomponents in it—will be completed as required. This technique was created for use in the development of the Polaris Missile Submarine. PERT is still used for very complex and more cutting-edge projects in which time estimates for things like breakthrough technologies are inherently more risky.

Components of Project Schedules

Project schedules have a number of components that make them up. Each component plays an important role in a schedule, and we review them in the following.

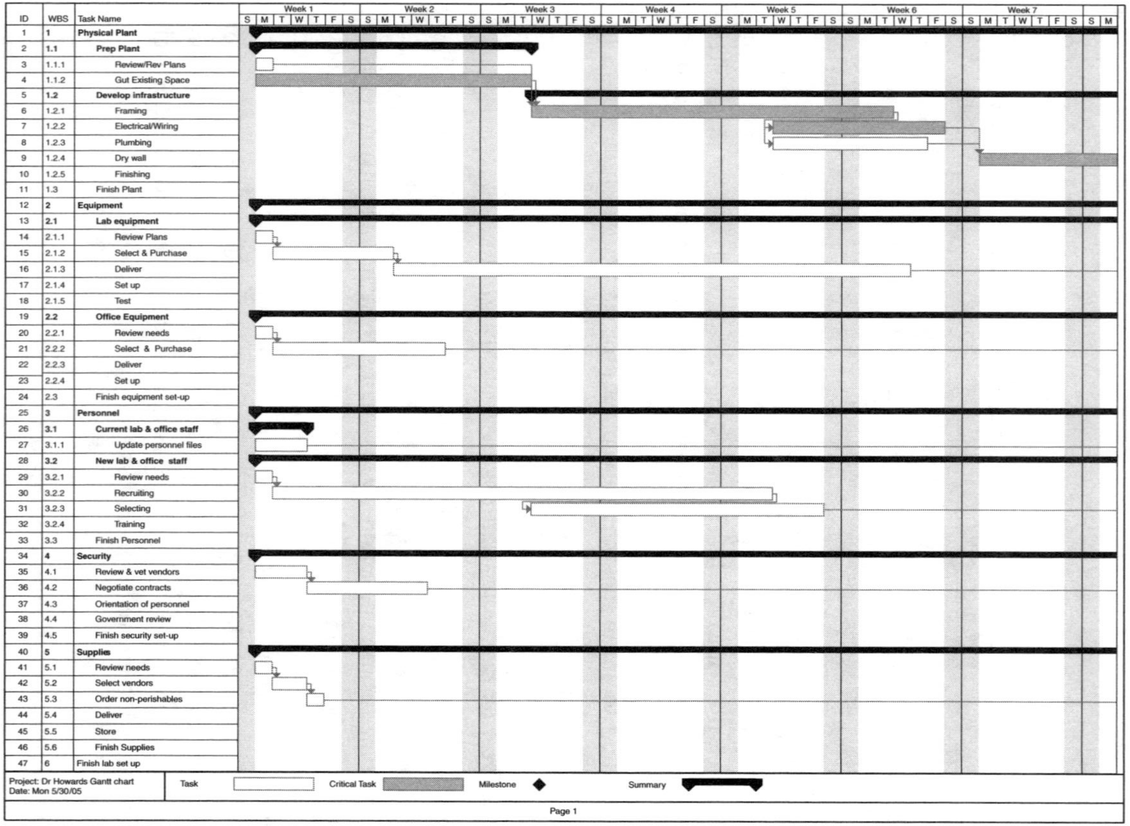

Figure 4.2 *(Continued)*

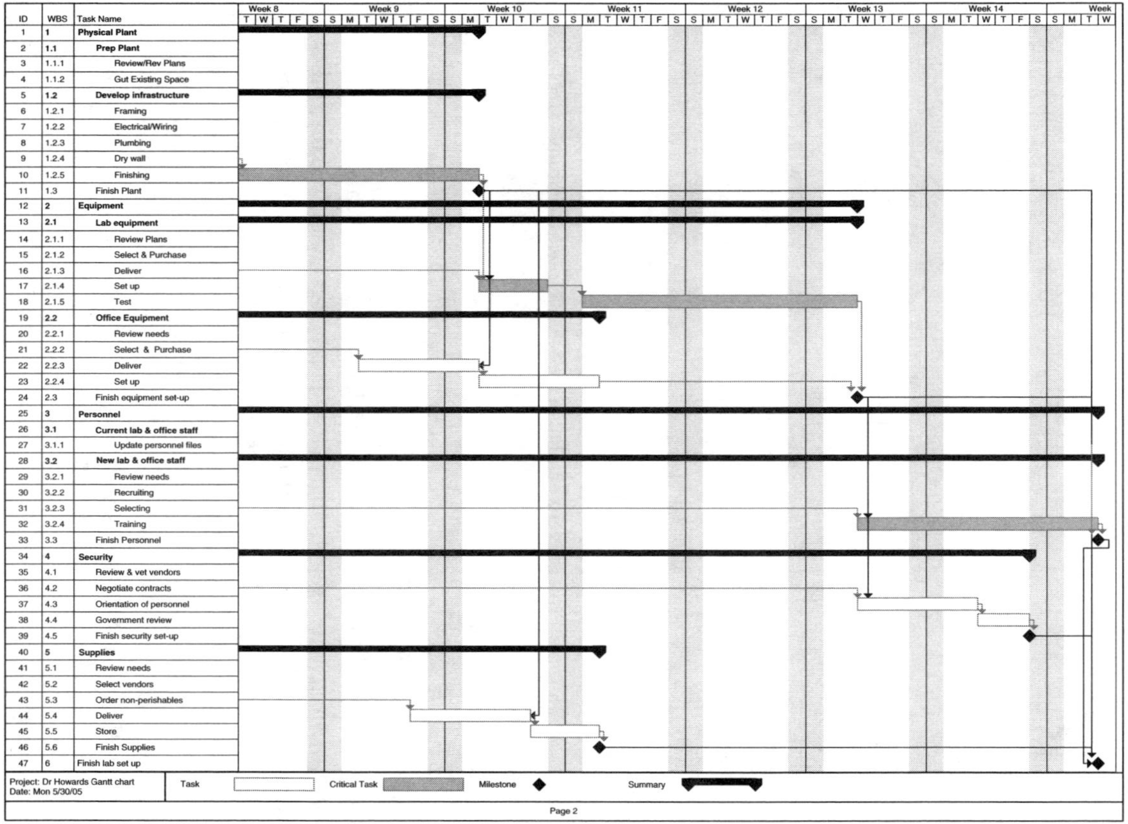

Figure 4.2   A Gantt Chart Illustrating Dr. Howard's Bio-Informatics Project

NOTE: Figure 4.2 was generated using Microsoft Project® 2000. WBS = Work breakdown structure.

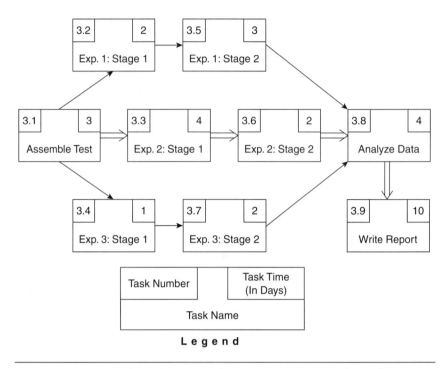

Figure 4.3   A Simple Project Network Diagram—Dr. Howard's Study

NOTE: Exp. = experiment.

Activities or Project Tasks

These are the tasks developed when producing a work breakdown structure (WBS). An activity is anything that will take time and, usually, other resources and money as well. Most often, activities are team tasks—those internal to the project itself. Sometimes, however, project activities include tasks that lie outside the project. For example, your boss, bank, or some regulator may have to approve something in your project before it can move forward. You want to make sure you include these kinds of external activities in your WBS and schedule as well.

Dependencies

Dependencies occur when one task is dependent on another task in some way. The most common form is the "finish-to-start" dependency, in which one or more predecessor tasks must finish before one or more succeeding tasks can begin. In Dr. Howard's Bio-Informatics Project (Figure 4.2), for example, he must finish selecting new laboratory personnel (3.2.3) before their training (3.2.4) can start. Three other less common dependencies are "start-to-start," "finish-to-finish," and "start-to-finish" dependencies. In a start-to-start dependency, two or more tasks must start at the same time. When Dr. Howard is actually conducting experiments, for example, he may have to start two or more of them at the same time to get valid results. In a finish-to-finish dependency, two or more tasks must finish at the same time. Although the delivery of equipment might begin at any time for Dr. Howard's lab, for example, it is scheduled to finish (i.e., be finally delivered to the site) when the lab itself is finished so it can be moved into it. Finally, a start-to-finish dependency signals that one or more tasks must start for one or more tasks to be finished.

Lag and Lead Times

Lag and lead times affect task dependencies in terms of the amount of time that must pass in one task before another task can be related to it. Lag time is the amount of time that must pass after work has been done on a task before work can start on a dependent, succeeding task. Concrete must cure for a while, for example, before anything can be built on it. Dr. Howard's study in Figure 4.3 may show another example of lag time. Each of the three experiments may require growing bacteria in petri dishes. It may take only half a day to set up the growth, but the remaining time in Stage 1 for each experiment may be needed for the growth to reach maturity for that particular line of bacteria.

Lead time means something very specific in project management. It means that a succeeding dependent task can begin before a preceding task has completely finished—it can "lead" the finish of the predecessor task. In the construction of Dr. Howard's lab (Figure 4.2), for example, the wiring (1.2.2) and plumbing (1.2.3) can begin before all the walls are put up (Framing, 1.2.1). If the walls take 15 days to complete, the wiring and plumbing might begin when two thirds of the walls are completed, thereby leading the completion by 5 days.

Milestones

Milestones are important events in the life of a project but consume no time or resources. They are usually added to a project schedule to signal when some component of the project should have been completed. In the Bio-Informatics Project shown in Figure 4.2, for example, every major project component (e.g., [1] Physical Plant, [2] Equipment) has a "finish" scheduled as a milestone (e.g., 1.3, 2.3, 3.3).[5]

The Project Network

Because a project ultimately depends on all project tasks being done at some point, all the project's activities and milestones will eventually be tied together in a network of project tasks. Figure 4.3 of Dr. Howard's study shows a network as it is commonly conceived. The Gantt chart in Figure 4.2, however, also shows the bio-informatics network as bars with arrows connecting them.

The Critical Path

Every project has a critical path—a sequence of tasks that will take longer to do than any other sequence of tasks. The project's critical path determines the earliest date the project can be completed. Because any change in the critical path affects the whole project, it commands a great deal of attention from project leaders. In planning, most risk assessments about the time it will take to do a task will be done along this path. If a leader wants to shorten the project completion date, he or she will work with the tasks scheduled along this path. When the project is being conducted, project leaders may take resources from an activity off the critical path and give them to an activity that is on the critical path to keep the project on schedule or to shorten the overall project—an activity known as "crashing."

The double-line arrows show the critical path in Dr. Howard's study in Figure 4.3. The critical path can also be shown in Gantt charts. In Figure 4.2, for example, the critical path is indicated by the solid bars in the diagram connectet to each other with arrows—those are the tasks that make up the critical path. They must start and end as scheduled for the project to finish on time.

Slack or Float

Tasks that lie off the critical path have "slack" or "float." Those tasks can begin later and finish later than scheduled without pushing back the completion time for the project as a whole. For example, take a look at the "Office Equipment" (2.2) task of selecting and purchasing of equipment (2.2.2) in the Gantt chart in Figure 4.2. It is scheduled to begin on the second day of the project and will be finished in the following week. Delivery (2.2.3) of the equipment, however, cannot begin until near the completion date of laboratory construction some eight weeks later. Selection and purchasing of office equipment, then, has a fair amount of slack. Dr. Howard may choose to put off that task until later and use its personnel for other, more pressing project work.

How to Develop a Project Schedule: Focus—Gantt Charts

The process for developing a project schedule can be broken down into five basic steps. First, the project itself needs to be broken down into its many activities. When building a Gantt chart, these need to be listed in an outline form. Second, task times need to be reviewed. Third, the dependency between those tasks needs to be determined—what needs to be done first, second, third, and the like, so that other tasks can follow and build on the initial ones. Fourth, the project network of tasks needs to be constructed. Fifth, the project's critical path needs to be determined. We cover these here with a focus on developing Gantt charts.

Break Down Project and Create an Outline of Tasks

The WBS covered in Chapter 3 will identify the tasks that need to be done in a project. To create a Gantt chart, those tasks need to be arranged in outline form. The bio-informatics' Gantt chart in Figure 4.2 provides a good example of a WBS in outline form in the chart's for left columns. The major divisions of the project are given the highest level numbers in the outline of project work (e.g., 1, 2, and 3 for Physical Plant, Equipment, and Personnel). The next division of work receives the next highest level of outline numbers (e.g., 1.2 and 1.3 for Prepare Plant and Develop Infrastructure). This outlining process continues until all project tasks are listed. The outline form helps keep similar, related tasks together.

Review Time Estimates

You may recall that when a WBS is developed, time estimates are also made for how long the individual tasks will take to complete. Those estimates should be reviewed prior to the schedule's construction, and should include such considerations as required lag time.[6] As was suggested in Chapter 3, it is a good idea to think about optimistic and pessimistic time estimates as well as your "best guess." The time risks of a project are a major threat to getting the project done on time and on budget and deserve extra attention.

Determine Dependencies

The next step to take is to determine how project tasks relate to one another—their dependencies. The most common dependency is the finish-to-start dependency—one task must finish before another can start.

I like to start this task by looking within project job categories first. For example, in the Bio-Informatics Project in Figure 4.2, attention might be given to the Physical Plant first and to its related tasks. It is because these tasks *are* related that dependencies are likely to occur among them. In a similar manner, a first pass would progress through all the other major project components.

Next, it is a good idea to step back a bit and consider how major project categories relate to one another. "Developing the Physical Plant" in the Bio-Informatics Project, for example, is necessary before most activities can occur within it. The last task of construction, then, needs to precede those follow-on, dependent activities.

Construct the Network of Project Activities

The next step is to construct the schedule network itself. In Gantt charts like that shown in Figure 4.2, each task in the work breakdown outline is given its own row, and the tasks are clustered into project components of related activities. The columns to the right of the task listing represent time intervals in a project—quite often, days of the week.[7]

Initially the major breakdowns are ignored, and focus is given to the individual tasks. Bars or lines are drawn to represent the amount of time needed for a task and are placed on the calendar appropriately. Task bars are placed at their earliest possible start dates, keeping in mind any tasks on which they depend.

When all lower order tasks are placed on the calendar, higher-order "summary bars" can be drawn completely encompassing the lower-order tasks that make them up. They visually summarize the project work beneath them.

Once all the bars are placed on the project calendar, arrows can be drawn from the end of a preceding task to the beginning of a successor task that depends on it. In Gantt charts, the arrow is drawn straight across the row of the preceding task before it connects with its successor task. The length of the arrow indicates the preceding task's float or slack, as shown in the Bio-Informatics Project in Figure 4.2.[8]

Determine the Critical Path

Finding a project's critical path is rather straightforward, but the calculations involved can become quite challenging in complex projects. Project management software provides the best solution to this task, but project leaders should have a basic understanding of the process involved.

Recall that the critical path is the longest sequence of activities from the beginning of a project to its end. Because, eventually, all activities are connected to both the beginning and the end of the project, one path will come up as the longest. The key to finding the critical path, then, is to trace the various paths of dependent activities in a project from its beginning to its end, always making sure to focus on the path that is taking the longest time to complete. To do so, one keeps adding the time it takes to do a task to the dependent task that comes next. Whenever two or more paths come together, one chooses the path with the longest time and begins tracing the next sequence of tasks from it, once again keeping track of the new task times that follow. Eventually, this process ends with the last project task sequence. This is known as a "forward pass" and results in two outcomes. The first is the amount of time it will take to finish the project—the sum of the longest sequence of task times. The second outcome is the identification of the longest sequence of tasks itself—the critical path. Any change in time for any of those tasks will affect the finish date of the project.

In critical path calculations, a "backward pass" is usually done as well. Beginning with the last task's finish date, task times are subtracted along task sequences. Doing so will indicate the amount of slack time between dependent tasks—none for those on the critical path and various amounts of slack for those tasks off the critical path. A more detailed description of the CPM is beyond the scope of this chapter, but Appendix A, "Calculating the Critical Path Using the Critical Path Method," demonstrates both the forward and backward pass and the calculations that result from them.

Using the Output of a Project Schedule

The project's work schedule plays a variety of roles for the project leader. These roles include helping visualize the project as whole, revising the project's estimates, and making project adjustments. Finally, because the schedule arranges project tasks through time, it allows project leaders to command, control, and coordinate resource use and outcomes of the project.

Visualizing the Project as a Whole

One of the most important benefits of the project schedule is that it provides a "whole picture" of the project. As we said in Chapter 3, the WBS provides a list of all the tasks and, if graphed appropriately, it can provide a picture of the project's structure as well (e.g., recall the Compliance Project graphed in Figure 3.1). The project's schedule, however, is the only tool that arranges the project's tasks through time. At first glance, the Gantt chart of the Bio-Informatics Project in Figure 4.2 might seem a bit confusing. Project leaders, staff, and others quickly come to read such schedules, however, like orchestra leaders and musicians read music. In fact, project schedules are designed, in part, to help project stakeholders do just that.

Project Phases

As one looks past the task "trees" to see the outlines of the project's "forest," the first pattern that begins to emerge is the phases of the project. All projects are composed of tasks done through time, and clusters of them often have to be done before other clusters. These task clusters form the various phases and subcomponents of a project. Different resources are likely to be needed in different phases, and each phase is likely to require different deliverables for the project as a whole. Who leads what activities may also change across project phases and project task clusters.

Project Dependencies

Another pattern that emerges from a project schedule is its network of task dependencies. These dependencies emerge as task "strings" through the project. The most commanding of these strings is the critical path—that sequence of tasks that determines the earliest completion date of the project. Possible project errors are riskier along this path because even a small problem here can affect the whole project. Tasks that lie off the critical path—although connected—are less critical to the timing of the project. Problems that occur with those tasks provide less risk to the project because their start and end dates are not as constrained. This slack in noncritical tasks provides "wiggle room" for the project and its leader. Project schedules help make these task dependencies and risks very clear.

Communication to Stakeholders

Because the project schedule provides a graphical arrangement of all the project tasks through time, it provides both a broad and a more detailed understanding of the project at the same time. As such, it makes for an excellent communication device for all stakeholders. The pace and timing of the project, for example, can be more easily communicated to clients. The most appropriate times for decision points, milestones, project reports, transfers of funds, and interim deliverables can be quickly and clearly communicated to clients with a project schedule. The project schedule is also useful in communicating with the host organization. When funds must flow to the project, when resources will be required, when updates make the most sense, and similar issues are all more clearly communicated with the help of project schedules. Finally, those working on the project also use the schedule as a principal aid in communication. Different people in the project team can see very clearly when their work must begin and end. They can also have a clear picture of the project as a whole in addition to their part of it. This allows them to see where their work fits in with the work of others and how it needs to be used. Internal and external suppliers also can see when their input is needed to make sure the right resources get to the right people at the right time.

Revision of Planning Assumptions and Estimates for the Project Plan

When a schedule is first produced, it aids in helping revise planning assumptions and estimates. The assumptions made and estimates given when the WBS is first developed are all done without formal regard to how the tasks are connected together through time. With the schedule developed, those estimates may need revision. Team members responsible for project components may well see tasks or entire task sequences that need to be added or others that are not needed at all. Project staff may also give more input into resource needs, personnel, time estimates, and dependencies between tasks when studying the schedule.

Internal and external resource suppliers can use the schedule to confirm availability of resources or discuss adjustments that need to be made. Project leaders themselves may well see things that they missed earlier in the planning phase. All changes, of course, have effects across the project. Because the schedule indicates what task sequences are most critical for getting the project done (e.g., those on the critical or near-critical paths[9]), particular attention can be given to the risk assessments of those tasks in particular.

Another assumption that needs to be checked is the level of resource use at any particular time in the project. In the initial WBS, resources are committed to tasks without regard to when they are to be used. When those tasks are scheduled at specific times, some resources may become overcommitted. Logistical problems may arise in the scheduling of equipment use and the flow of material. Personnel may also be overcommitted. It may be that some team members are scheduled to work more than 40 hours per week once tasks are arranged across time. Adjustments made in noncritical tasks with slack can help address this problem.

Project leaders typically spend a great deal of time revising and modifying the initial schedule to address issues and problems such as these. In truth, addressing all these matters can be quite frustrating. Project leaders need to keep in mind, however, that the only issue is when these issues and problems will be confronted—now in planning or later when they will cost more time, money, and headaches.

Making Adjustments to the Plan Throughout the Project

Because projects are unique endeavors, leaders often find that adjustments need to be made to keep the project on schedule and on budget while the project is under way. Project schedules allow project leaders to see the effects of any adjustments they make. The effects of adjustments can be seen even more clearly when using project management software. When resources are moved and times adjusted, the program can instantaneously update the resource use listings and the schedule, showing any changes in the critical path.

Project leaders quite often take resources from activities off the critical path and commit them to tasks on the critical path to help them reduce project risk, shorten project time, or keep the project on schedule if it is falling behind. If the project budget is in trouble, project leaders tend to look to tasks off the critical path for cutbacks. Although this is an acceptable approach to making needed adjustments, there are a number of problems that can emerge if the project leader is not careful.

First, resource shifts may lengthen other project tasks to the extent that a new critical path is developed. If a noncritical activity has only one day of slack, for example, shifting resources from it may well lengthen its time horizon beyond that one day, making it critical (e.g., the plumbing task [1.2.3] in Figure 4.2 becomes concurrently critical with the addition of a single day and pushes the whole project back if it takes any longer). For these reasons, project leaders often conduct "sensitivity analyses" on their critical paths. One approach is to shorten time estimates of activities on the critical path to see if other task sequences become critical. Another approach is to lengthen task estimates of tasks off the critical path to see if their task sequences then become critical.

A second problem that can emerge is an overuse of resources. It is not unusual, for example, that a member of the project team is working on several project tasks or both project and nonproject tasks at the same time. Looking at the work he or she is doing on only one project task can lead to the mistaken notion that the member can work elsewhere, resulting in overload. The same kind of overloading problem can arise with equipment and other resources. Careful tracking of scheduled resource use can help address this risk.

Finally, a problem emerges with what might be called "resource mathematics." Doubling the number of people working on a task, for example, rarely cuts task time in half. This is the case for at least two reasons. One is that increasing the number of personnel creates process loss. Problems with coordination, information sharing, "free riding," and the like tend to increase with more personnel. Another reason is that resources are often not smoothly interchangeable. It takes time to get up to speed, for example, when working on a new job. In addition, the knowledge, skills, and abilities of the new personnel may not be well fitted to the job requirements.

Command and Control

Still another key benefit of the project schedule is its use as a tool for project control. As a project network moves through time, a variety of project tasks must be done and resources used. Schedules help leaders manage those activities by clearly showing what tasks are currently in progress, who is working on them, and how close they should be to completion. Depending on the task's slack, project leaders know how much attention should be given to its on-time completion. As resources are used by the project, leaders can keep track and compare them to what was budgeted to keep control of project costs. (One tool used for cost control making use of the schedule is Earned Value Analysis and is discussed in Appendix B.)

Schedules also let leaders look forward into the near and farther term future of their projects. Armed with the knowledge of what will be required, leaders can ensure resources are available, adjust schedules and tasks, and anticipate, analyze, and address potential problems. Table 4.1 presents a list of questions project leaders can ask themselves as they move through the process of creating a schedule. Although not exhaustive, it can provide a check-off list of some key things to consider.

Table 4.1   Schedule Check-Off List

Depending on its complexity, a schedule can be a difficult tool to construct. Without a schedule, though, leaders cannot manage their projects. Listed here are a few key questions leaders should ask themselves as they move through the process of constructing a schedule. The questions are meant to encourage project leaders to think through the issues involved and to be used as a point of departure, and leaders should add other questions as they see fit. The assumption made here is that the schedule will be in the form of a Gantt chart and that a critical path will be developed.

(Continued)

Table 4.1 (Continued)

- Have all the core and support activities been included in the schedule? Have they been grouped together along work process lines and arranged appropriately in an outline form?

- Have all other scheduled work tasks been included? Consider the initiation and delivery of outsourced work. Consider regulatory reviews if required.

- Have task time estimates been reviewed and confirmed? Have they been properly represented in the schedule?

- Have lag times been incorporated into those tasks that require them? Consider any task that needs time to rest or mature after active work has finished. Consider adding lag times to such things as vendor delivery schedules.

- Have all task dependencies been included and reviewed in the schedule?

- Can some dependent tasks incorporate lead time? Is it possible for a dependent task to begin before its preceding task is complete?

- Have project milestones been placed appropriately in the project schedule? Consider locating them at times of project component reviews and completions. Will milestones require reviews or reports? If so, schedule the required tasks and include them in the WBS, budget, and related planning documents.

- Has a critical path been determined? Have near-critical activities been identified?

- Has task slack of noncritical project tasks been determined?

- Does the visual layout of the project schedule make sense? Is there initial "face validity" to the way tasks are arranged through time? Does the schedule communicate to the leader and to others the overall flow of the project in ways that will make sense to them? Consider whether work processes are clustered together in ways that make sense to those who work in and interact with them. Consider whether project phases make sense. Consider project dependencies between large project components as well as specific work tasks.

- Have resource requirements been arranged according to their scheduled use? Are any resources over- or undercommitted? Consider the workweeks and workloads of all project personnel. Consider the logistical requirements of all equipment and materials needed. Have arrangements been scheduled for their on-time delivery? Have any project task requirements of those arrangements been scheduled?

- Has the project budget been arranged in accordance with the project schedule of resource use? How easy is it to determine whether the project is on budget at any particular time during the project?

Summary

Project schedules are basic and invaluable tools for project planning and management. At its most basic, a project schedule is simply an arrangement of project tasks across time. Different kinds of schedules help project leaders build on this fundamental notion. Gantt or bar charts use bars to represent project activities, with the length of the bar representing the length of the activity. These bars are then placed on a project calendar to show start and end times at certain dates. The CPM is a kind of network diagram that helps project leaders determine a project's critical path and the slack of those tasks that do not lie on that path. The PERT accounts for time risks in projects by incorporating optimistic and pessimistic time estimates for tasks in addition to their likely completion times.

Project schedules have a number of components in common. All have project activities or tasks that are scheduled to begin and end at certain times. Most have milestones that represent important events in the life of a project. Whether shown on a schedule or not, project tasks are tied together by their dependencies—one must end, for example, before another can begin. Eventually, all project tasks are linked in some fashion, and those linkages can be represented in a project network of task dependencies shown by arrows connecting dependent tasks. One particular sequence of dependent tasks represents the critical path of a project—that sequence of tasks determines the earliest date the project can end. The dependent tasks on the critical path must begin and end no later than scheduled or the project gets pushed back. All other tasks have some degree of float or slack—their start and finish times can vary to some extent without the project completion date being affected.

Project schedules are constructed from the activities in the WBS, their time estimates, and their dependencies on one another. The first step in developing a Gantt chart is to break down the project's work and arrange it in outline form on a spreadsheet. The rows of the spreadsheet will be dedicated to the project's tasks and the columns to the project calendar—most often representing days. Second, time estimates for each task are made and reviewed. Third, task dependencies are determined. Fourth, the Gantt chart is built by constructing and placing bars for each activity on the spreadsheet. The length of each bar is constructed to be as long as the time estimate of the task. It is placed by putting it where the task is to begin on the project calendar. Dependent tasks do not begin until their predecessor tasks are completed as required. Gantt charts often connect their bars with arrows showing task dependencies as well.

A project schedule serves a variety of purposes. One is that it helps the project leader to visualize the project as a whole with its various phases and dependencies. It also helps other stakeholders to visualize the project and serves as an excellent communication device to the project's clients, its host organization, and others. Another use of the project schedule is to help in the revision of project assumptions and estimates. Once it is seen as a whole, various stakeholders can review the tasks, assumptions, and estimates to assess any problems, additions, or opportunities for the project. The project schedule also is critical in project revisions and adjustments. From initial planning to the ending of a project, leaders are called on to make adjustments of one sort or another. The project schedule helps guide such adjustments by making clear how they affect other tasks, resources, and project time. Finally, project schedules play an important role in command and control of the project. They help project leaders focus their attention on critical tasks and resources as the project moves forward and allow them to keep track of how the project is progressing and using its available resources.

Review Questions

1. What is a project schedule?

2. Describe the three kinds of scheduling techniques covered in this chapter.

3. What are the components of project schedules covered in this chapter?

4. Define and give examples of dependent tasks.

5. Define and give examples of tasks with lag and lead times.

6. Define and give examples of tasks that have float or slack in relation to other tasks.

7. What is a project's critical path? What role does the critical path play in project management?

8. Describe the process of developing a project schedule. Use either the Gantt chart or the CPM technique in your discussion.

9. What are the ways project schedules are used in projects?

Exercise

1. Work individually or as a team to develop a WBS. In this exercise, you will build a Gantt chart.[10]

    a. Focus on a project that is relevant to you or your team.

    b. Develop a WBS for a significant portion of your project (if you developed a WBS for Chapter 3, use it for this exercise if you wish).

    c. Display the WBS in outline form on sheets of graph paper (if you are using project management software, display the tasks in it). Leave a few rows above your WBS outline.

    d. On a row above the beginning of the WBS, start numbering columns to the left of the WBS. These columns will represent the days of your project from Day One to the final day.

    e. Estimate the time required to complete each task.

    f. Determine any dependencies between tasks.

    g. Draw a line to the left of each task representing the time it will take to accomplish. Begin with the first tasks that can be done. Start dependent tasks where required preceding tasks have ended.

    h. Continue building your Gantt chart, keeping in mind dependencies and lag times.

    i. When you are done, evaluate the project network you have created. Identify needs for required modification and opportunities to shorten the schedule.

Endnotes

1. The Graphical Evaluation and Review Technique is a fourth scheduling technique. It allows feedback loops and conditional branching but will not be covered here.

2. This sequence of tasks is shown without regard to the other tasks in the larger project shown in Figure 4.2.

3. This is called an activity-on-node diagram because the activity or task is displayed in the nodes of the network. There are also activity-on-arrow diagrams, in which the task is labeled on the arrow instead of in the node. These are used far less frequently.

4. Monte Carlo simulation is named after Monte Carlo gambling wheels. Each "spin of the wheel" assumes a particular start and end date for project tasks. Computers can spin the wheel thousands of times very quickly and calculate the likely distribution of project times between the beginning and end of a project or the sequence of tasks within it. This is beyond the scope of this book, however.

5. Often, milestones include some report or other deliverable to the client or to another stakeholder. If so, then it is important to remember that this kind of milestone must be preceded by activities that produce whatever is needed for the

milestone and that they be included in the work breakdown structure, schedule, cost estimates, and the like.

6. I like to include lag time for such things as vendor delivery of purchases, inspectors showing up once notified, and the like.

7. The project calendar in Figure 4.2 shows Saturdays and Sundays, as well as the days of the normal workweek. I like to include them to help visually keep track of the weeks in a project. They are not counted as project work time, however.

8. When doing this by hand, arrows are usually optional. In more complex projects, they add valuable visual information and are easily constructed with project management software. In fact, modern project management software can make the process of developing project schedules a fairly easy one. Microsoft Project®, for example, facilitates constructing a work breakdown structure, estimating activity times, drawing bars, linking them with arrows, and placing them on a project calendar all at the same time when developing a Gantt chart. The Gantt chart of the Bio-Informatics Project in Figure 4.2, for example, is based on the output of Microsoft Project 2000®.

9. A near-critical path is a sequence of tasks that are close to becoming critical. More attention is given to this issue shortly.

10. This exercise is designed to produce a Gantt chart. The exercise assumes that the reader is not using project management software. If the reader is using project software, disregard references to using graph paper and so forth. Instead of graph paper, spreadsheet programs can be used if project management software is unavailable.

5

Developing Project Teams

Introduction	82
The Achievement Project	82
Chapter Overview	82
What Is a Team?	83
What Is a Successful Team?	84
Successful Teams Deliver the Goods	84
Successful Teams Get Better	84
Successful Teams Are Satisfied and Committed	85
Fundamentals of Team Structure	86
Team Size	86
Team Composition	86
Team Governance	87
Team Identity	88
Team Interactions	88
Team Ideology	89
Norms	90
Roles	90
Goals	92
Team Development	92
Forming	92
Storming	93
Norming	94

Performing	94
Adjourning	94
Summary	95
Review Questions	97
Exercises	97
Endnotes	99
Table 5.1: Comparison Issues for Best and Worst Teams	98

Introduction

The Achievement Project

Leanne Phillips was more than a little concerned. She had just been put in charge of a tough and politically sensitive project for the Los Padres School District. Recent changes in federal regulations for school districts nationwide required that students demonstrate certain levels of achievement across a number of academic areas for the schools to receive continued funding. Like many school districts across the country, Los Padres had a good but still spotty record of achievement. Some students, particularly those from poorer areas of the district, had continuing difficulty in reaching the achievement levels mandated. This would mean loss in funding if it continued and, in particularly difficult schools, even more drastic action.

Ms. Phillips had worked for the district for a number of years and had tracked these changes in federal regulations since they were first developed. The board of supervisors had now called on her to lead a project to address the problem. They wanted her to identify the most critical issues involved in the problem, develop the information they would need to understand and address those issues, and make recommendations about courses of action the board should take. Leanne had an excellent reputation with the board, and she intended to use it to get the resources and help she needed. Along these lines, she realized that she would need an exceptional project team to pull this project off well. The problem of just how to put together such a team began to nag at her.

Chapter Overview

Like many people, Leanne Phillips had worked in countless teams. Some of them worked well, but most really did not live up to what she considered true team commitment and success. It seemed that the usual way teams were created was to assemble a bunch of people, say they were now a team, and that was that. She realized that she needed to do far more than that, but she had trouble identifying the most important factors to consider in assembling and developing a team such as the one she would need.

Unfortunately, there is no prescription for constructing perfect teams. There are, however, a set of key success factors project leaders like Leanne should consider in developing them. This chapter is devoted to reviewing and discussing some of the most important ones. We begin by addressing just what a team *is*. There is a lot of disagreement over the term, and we need to anchor our discussion of what is really meant by the idea of a team. We then move on to consider what counts for team success. If leaders want successful teams, they need to know where they are aiming. Next, we examine some of the more critical factors that underpin successful teams. Armed with such knowledge, project leaders can avoid some of the more common problems associated with poorly performing teams. Finally, we examine how teams develop from just a collection of people into a fully functioning team and what they need from project leaders to do so.

What Is a Team?

There is a lot of disagreement about just what constitutes a team. The term has been used to refer to any number of groups—from small work groups to entire organizations. In this chapter, we have in mind a specific type of workgroup best defined by Katzenbach and Smith in a *Harvard Business Review* article.[1] They described a team as a small number of people with complementary skills who are committed to a common purpose, a common set of performance goals, and a common approach for which they hold themselves mutually accountable.

Katzenbach and Smith[2] highlighted a number of important team characteristics that we will explore later. The first is that teams are usually made up of a small number of team members. As teams become large, they tend to stop acting like a team. A second characteristic is that team members do different kinds of tasks requiring different kinds of knowledge and skills. So-called "synergy" comes from different team members doing different tasks in a coordinated way. To achieve that coordination, different team members must assume work roles that fit together so that the work of one team member fits well with the work of others. A third characteristic is one of direction: Teams have a common purpose and a common set of performance goals. Teams know where they are headed and what must be produced. Fourth, teams have a common "game plan" for how they will achieve their goals. Finally, team activities and performance are controlled. The control of true teams comes from within them— team members hold one another mutually accountable. They review their progress, assess their performance, maintain or alter their plans, and reward and discipline their members to achieve their common goals.

Our focus will be on this kind of team. Even with such a focus, however, looking at project teams is something of a challenge. By far, most of the work done on teams has been oriented to ongoing workgroups—not the kind of temporary teams found in project environments. What we know about the structure, composition, and dynamics of teams, then, will need to be examined with an eye toward the realities and needs of project teams.

What Is a Successful Team?

Research on team effectiveness has used a number of criteria for team success.[3] Three of the most important are considered here. They include success in producing client deliverables, promoting team development, and developing team commitment.

Successful Teams Deliver the Goods

For a project team to be a success, it must, first and foremost, "deliver the goods." In project teams, that means producing the project's deliverables according to specification, on time, and on budget. That said, in project work, the goods to deliver often require a great deal of leader attention.

Clarifying a project's mission, objectives, and deliverables is a critical early task for any project leader, and we devoted considerable time to it in Chapter 2. Like many other project leaders, Leanne Phillips is likely to find this a particularly challenging task. Initially, she will work with her principal client—the board of supervisors—to clarify project objectives and deliverables.

Leanne will soon find, however, that other stakeholders will develop expectations about what the project should produce and how it should be conducted. These other stakeholders will also have some say in determining the extent to which the project is considered a success. Leanne will need the board to champion and support her project. But that likely will not be enough. She will also have to manage the expectations of the other critical stakeholders—a topic we address at length in Chapter 6.

Successful Teams Get Better

A successful project team is also one that gets better over time. One of the nice things about human capital—unlike most any other kind of capital—is that it can get *better* with use and *increase* rather than diminish in value.

Teams should get better, in at least two ways. First, team members should get better in terms of their knowledge, skills, and abilities to produce project deliverables. Second, they should get better at working as a team. Team skills are often overlooked yet are essential to successful teams. A simple, conscious attention to developing both task and team skills will go a long way toward team development.

Because project teams are generally thought of as temporary, some leaders may underestimate the value of developmental needs. Many project teams, however, are not so temporary at all. Some teams remain together for years across the life of a large project. Other project teams remain together across a number of different projects (e.g., audit or consulting teams). Still other project teams evolve into permanent work teams once their project is done (e.g., teams brought together to effect some organizational change of which they will be a part). Attention to team development in all these cases will prove to be a wise investment.

Even with truly temporary project teams, however, there is reason to attend to developmental needs. Project leaders often find that they deal with many of the same personnel over a number of projects. Attending to their development not only helps the larger organization but is a good investment in the leader's own future projects. Team members also tend to be more satisfied and committed to project leaders who show their developmental commitment to them.[4] Finally, attention to team development will pay off in the shorter as well as longer term. Team members can climb project learning curves faster with development and turn their increased satisfaction and commitment to project needs.

Developmental efforts can take many forms, but one is particularly appropriate for project work. It is simply to confront and work through project challenges as they arise. Project leaders are well advised to use their teams to periodically review the project and confront project problems as they occur. Quite often, teams can spot and solve problems better than individuals working alone—even experienced project leaders. In so doing, teams can get better at project work and leaders can get a double benefit—team development and good advice on project challenges.

Successful Teams Are Satisfied and Committed

The final criterion of team success is the extent to which team members are satisfied and committed to one another, the team, and the project on which they work. During the life of the project, satisfaction and commitment is seen in the amount of effort and persistence team members make toward team goals. It is seen in the amount of team cohesion as well. After the project is over, satisfaction and commitment can continue to express themselves in a desire to work with the same team members and the project leader if the opportunity arises.

Fundamentals of Team Structure

Project leaders like Leanne Phillips should consider at least six fundamental team factors when building, developing, and leading teams. Three focus on construction characteristics: team size, team composition, and team governance. The others focus more on factors that affect how team members see and deal with themselves as a team: developing a team identity, team interactions, and important components of what is called a "team ideology."

Team Size

Although there may be no theoretical upper limit to the size of a team, there seems to be a practical one for at least two reasons. First, as teams grow in size, they tend to break down into smaller "social-psychological" groups who see themselves attached more to one another in smaller informal groups to which they have been assigned. Second, as teams grow in size, their internal dynamics become cumbersome. They begin to experience what is known as "process loss."[5] As size increases, it becomes more and more difficult to coordinate actions, communicate effectively, adjust to changes in plans, and the like. It also becomes easier to let others do the work, resulting in what economists call "free riding" and social psychologists call "social loafing." Experienced project leaders know full well, for example, that doubling the size of a project team most often does *not* double output or cut project time in half!

What is the magic number? No one can really say, and it probably depends on the nature of the work a team is doing and how well the members work together. The law of diminishing returns on team size, however, begins to kick in early, and a project leader will most certainly see the effects as team size moves into the teens.

Team Composition

Team composition refers to just who should be on a project team. The chief considerations for team membership are the knowledge, skills, and abilities to do the project's work. One cluster of these items needed for project work are those required to produce the project's deliverables. Most often, these skills are technical in nature. Another cluster of skills are the social or people skills needed to keep a team working together and to help connect its work with various external constituencies. Team members who can get along and work through stressful situations, for example, are an important asset. When project tasks require contact with clients, managers in the host organization, or other important stakeholders, having the interpersonal skills to do so well can also be critical to a team's success.[6] A third cluster of skills needed to do the project's work are managerial and leadership skills. Project work needs to be planned, organized, and executed in effective and efficient ways. Project members quite often look to project leaders for these skills, but the more they are distributed within the project team, the more the project leader can turn over team activities to the team itself.

Team Governance

The amount of control a team has over its own project management is also an important factor to consider. Team control can vary a great deal. At one extreme are manager-led teams that have little control at all. They are told what to do and how to do it. It may well be that there are a number of ongoing teams that work for the Los Padres School District that fit this description. When they first form, project teams tend to be manager led because the project leader plays a more directive role in laying out the project and launching project work. Manager-led teams can be quite successful in achieving whatever goals and objectives are assigned to them. As teams mature, however, they can get better at what they do and address a wider range of challenges if they can develop into self-managed work teams.

Self-managed work teams have more control over their operations. They are given their objectives but how they achieve them is up to the team members. Leanne Phillips may well develop some of her project teams along these lines. A team whose objective is to investigate the federal regulations that are affecting the district might develop into such a team. They would be tasked, for example, to investigate and report on the regulations, how they have been implemented, and how the federal courts have interpreted them. How they would do so, however, would be left up to them as a team. To be successful, self-managed work teams need to have the knowledge, skills, abilities, and resources to manage themselves and do project work. They need the authority to make their own operational decisions and, of course, they need commitment to project goals as well.

Self-directed and self-governing teams are two other kinds of team governance systems, but they are rarely seen in project or other organizational work. Self-directed teams have control over the choice of team objectives as well as team operations. Once launched, project teams are usually given their objectives as well as their required deliverables. Early in the project initiation process, however, project leaders may have some voice in establishing or defining project objectives, and they would be well advised to do so. Leanne Phillips, for example, has been given a mission and three broad objectives: identify critical issues, develop requisite information, and provide recommendations for action to the board. She should take this opportunity, however, to help define her project objectives and deliverables more specifically and get board endorsement of them.

Finally, self-governing teams determine their own missions and how to accomplish them. They are typically located only at the top of organizational hierarchies and almost never found as project teams. The board of supervisors, for example, might operate as a self-governing team.[7]

Team Identity

Effective teams also need a team identity.[8] Members need to see themselves as a team separate and distinct from other people and teams. This means that teams need to have firm boundaries. Firm boundaries promote team cohesion and the development of commitment. Just as important, people outside the team see it as a team and treat it as such. They know where they can go to get project business done and which teams have legitimate claim over project-relevant resources.

Team identities can be developed any number of ways. "Co-locating" team members in the same physical setting will tend to foster a perception of "we-ness" among them and a "they-ness" toward those outside. Team names also tend to foster a team identity. The "steering committee," the "Achievement Project team," and the "Upper Westside Parent's Group" are all examples of teams that may play some role in the Achievement Project. Their names help them define who they are and what they do—for themselves as well as others with whom they deal.

Team Interactions

Team members need to interact with one another to get project work done. The modes and styles of team interaction have taken on new importance as older forms have given way to newer ones. Traditional project teams were typically located together. Their basic form of interaction was face-to-face. Newer forms of communications and interaction have allowed the development of virtual teams.[9] Unbounded by geography, team members use a wide array of digital communications to interact with one another.

With virtual teams, project leaders can tap human resources from around the world, and they use a wide variety of project management software to help them do so. Even traditional teams working closely together now use digital communications to interact with one another more effectively.

The most potent form of interaction, however, remains face-to-face interaction for at least two reasons. First, face-to-face interaction allows for far richer forms of communication. A wider variety of nonverbal communication can occur face to face, for example, than can occur with most digital forms of communication. Body language, tone of voice, pauses, and the like all add to the richness of communication team members can experience. Second, face-to-face interaction facilitates the exercise of group pressure far more than digital interaction. Team members get a deeper feeling for what the team considers more important when dealing with one another face to face.

As face-to-face interaction is replaced with other means of interaction, the team begins to lose this richness of interaction and power of physical presence. Voice-only communications like phone conferences filter out body language. E-mails filter out pauses, intonations, and a sense of what the other person is feeling. Asynchronous communications make it difficult to get the immediate feedback needed to keep communications and interactions accurate, effective, and efficient.

The means and modes of digital communication and virtual interactions have added a great deal of potential to project work. As they develop, they will surely add more. Face-to-face interactions, however, will likely remain the richer and more potent form of communication, and the project leader is wise to build in and budget for them at critical junctures in the project.

It is likely that Leanne Phillips will want to have face-to-face interactions, for example, with her own core project team and with critical stakeholder groups around the district. Initial meetings and important milestones should command face-to-face interactions as well. Certainly, as unanticipated problems arise over project goals or the appropriate means to achieve them, face-to-face interactions will allow for richer communications and a more open negotiating venue.

Team Ideology

Effective teams have a common team ideology. By ideology, I mean that team members have common ideas about things important to the team. What constitutes appropriate and inappropriate team behavior, who should be doing what and how, and what the team is trying to achieve, for example, are all critical components of a team's ideology. Although team members will be engaged in different tasks, may be located in different locations, or face unexpected problems and opportunities, the more they share common ideas about the team and how it works, the more they will think and react as a cohesive, coordinated unit.[10]

Although the ideas team members have about the team can vary widely, three critical kinds of ideas deserve special attention: ideas about team norms, team roles, and team goals.

Norms

Norms are the rules teams develop about how their members should act—what is acceptable and what is not. Although teams can adopt norms from outside the team, most often they rise from the common expectations team members have of one another. Quite often, teams are unaware of their own norms until they are pointed out or someone violates them.

Norms are the principal means teams use to govern themselves—to hold themselves mutually accountable. Teams can control themselves to the extent that team members have clear expectations of one another and have both the means and the will to enforce those expectations.

Effective teams tend to adopt and enforce a few pivotal norms.[11] In project teams, these include norms covering the project's deliverables and how they should be produced. Norms about what constitutes proper team behavior with regard to the project and to one another are other kinds of critical norms that should be considered.

Like any project leader, Leanne Phillips should address pivotal project norms early in the life of her project. Giving key norms explicit attention will help her team establish the policies and procedures needed for its own command and control system.

Roles

A defining characteristic of any team is that its members do different tasks. To be successful, the results or output of those tasks must come together into a coherent product or service. For all this to happen, team members must perform different roles that fit together well.

Team roles are like roles in a play. They are the behaviors team members must perform for the team to have a successful "production." The team's "task roles" attend to the production of the project's products and services. "People," "socio-emotional," or "maintenance" roles attend to keeping everyone working together well. Finally, "leadership" or "managerial" roles attend to the management and organizational needs of the project and keeping it on track. Unlike roles in a play, team roles are not defined by scriptwriters and clarified by directors. Team roles arise from the often unspoken expectations of team members themselves.

When a team works well together, its members perform the roles that are needed, when they are needed, and in ways that are needed. Although this is easy to say, it is often difficult to accomplish for a number of reasons. First, important roles are often overlooked. This is less of a problem with task roles because the project's objectives and work breakdown structure tend to focus attention on them. Leadership and managerial roles, however, tend to get less attention. What the leader expects from the team and what the team can expect from the leader are role elements that often go unexpressed. The roles leaders will play in decisionmaking, providing close or loose supervision, providing training, and the like are generally ignored until problems arise. "People" roles are the most overlooked. Little express attention is paid to what is expected in terms of cooperating, handling conflict, facilitating participation, addressing what constitutes appropriate team citizenship, and the like until conflicts demand their attention.

A second problem with proper role play is that different people have different expectations of role holders. Almost always, this leads to increases in conflict and losses in team performance. The different and conflicting expectations experienced by project leaders is a case in point. When teams first come together, their members typically have very different preferences and expectations of the project manager. So do clients, managers in the host organization, and other external stakeholders. In a similar way, team members have differing expectations of one another that often cause problems in role performance.

The third problem in role performance arises when role holders do not have the full range of knowledge, skills, and abilities to perform their roles well. Generally, a fair amount of attention is given to the skills needed to perform the task roles of a project. Far less attention is usually given to the skills needed to perform people roles and, surprisingly, leadership roles as well.

Early in the life cycle of any new project, team members need to come to a common understanding about how important roles in a project are to be played and who will play them. This can be done in at least two ways. First, time can be set aside to discuss critical team roles as a team topic in itself. What the team can expect from its leader and from one another are two role topics that warrant discussion early in any project. Second, the discussion of roles themselves should be considered a legitimate and important topic to address as problems with roles—that is, team member expectations of one another—emerge. When roles are given early and continuing attention as needed, role performance will increase along with project performance.

Goals

A common understanding about the overall purpose of the project and its specific deliverables is one of the most important factors in a team's success. Goals give common direction to a team. The more specific the goals are, the more specific is the direction.

The goal specification process in project management attends well to this issue (see Chapter 2). Specifying the project's mission, its objectives and deliverables, and the task objectives needed to produce them all combine to provide a good goal structure to a project. The next need, then, is for the project team to develop a common understanding of the goal structure and how the product of their work fits into it. Meetings early in the project cycle covering the goal structure and how it was produced will go a long way toward producing the common understanding of project goals needed for project work.

Team Development

Project teams form anew with each new project. At first, the team is simply a collection of individuals in a project group. For these groups to become project teams, they need to go through a developmental process.[12] Team development has been studied from a variety of perspectives, but one has received the most attention: the "stage model" of team development developed by Tuckman and Jensen.[13] This model breaks the development of teams into five stages: forming, storming, norming, performing, and adjourning. Project leaders can help their teams develop more quickly when they are aware of these stages and the team's developmental needs in each phase.

Forming

When project groups first form, their members are unclear about the goals and priorities of the project ahead and the roles they will play. As with many first introductions, members also tend to be polite and cautious, and to monitor their comments and behaviors. They tend to go along with most of what is being said as they try to feel one another out. If they have disagreements or concerns, they tend to hold back on their comments.

At this early stage, the team needs to have the project's goals clarified as well as the basic plans to achieve them. Members will also want to know what task roles they will play and how they are expected to play them. This is a good time, too, to address some of the more important, pivotal norms that will be used to govern project behaviors.

The cautious politeness that characterizes the forming stage has at least two other implications for project leadership. The first is that most team members tend to defer to those who are more dominant. Some project members may use this opportunity to assert their own ideas and begin to take over project discussions and decisionmaking. Project leadership is a central concern to the team at this stage, and although project participation is welcomed, the project leader needs to establish command of the project team from the very beginning. This is accomplished by demonstrating an in-depth knowledge of the project and its need, a command of team process, and a comfortable assumption of one's own project authority.

A second implication for leadership in the forming stage is that project leaders often find that team members will tend to agree with a most anything they say. Leaders should be aware, however, that this "silent affirmation" might be due to members simply holding back, as is characteristic of this stage. The stresses and strains of the project itself may soon call into question early work in team development.

Storming

The storming stage is characterized by open or covert conflict over project issues. The term *storming* tends to evoke mental images of thunder and lightning. Some teams may exhibit this kind of conflict but most do not. Teams go through a storming stage simply because different people have different ideas about the project and how it should be run. These differences begin to emerge once the honeymoon of the forming stage is over and people feel freer to express their opinions.

One common response to differing ideas among team members is to share them with one or two others who may hold similar views. In this way, larger project teams break into smaller, informal subgroups whose members tend to see things the same way but differently from other groups. Left unaddressed for too long, disagreements between subgroups can erupt into the kind of open conflict for which this stage is named. At this point, struggles for power can emerge, communications suffer, and project work slow down and become uncoordinated.

Project leaders should not be surprised when disagreements emerge within the team. If they remain covert, the leader may even want to probe for them for at least two reasons. First, different views can bring with them good ideas about the project and how it might be run. Although snap decisions about project changes should be avoided, leaders should be open to new and better ways to run the project.[14] Second, when disagreements are found, they are more easily resolved earlier rather than later in the project.

Although team members may disagree about one or another aspect of the project, most simply want their ideas considered and resolved. The team tends to look to the project leader to play the lead role in resolving differences, and members will generally defer to the leader if they believe their views have been given due consideration.[15]

Norming

Norming is the stage in which project members come to understand and accept the norms of the project, its goals, and one another's roles. Although everyone may not be in 100% agreement with all project particulars, the team has come to a common understanding and acceptance of the project and how it is to be run. Noticeable characteristics of this stage are team cohesion and commitment to the project and its objectives.

Performing

The performing stage is when the team begins to act like a team. Their work is well coordinated, and they have learned to deal with problems productively as they arise. Decisions about project work are given to those best able to make them and project work to those best skilled to do it.

As the team moves through the norming and performing stages, less supervision is needed because the team itself is taking on some important elements of the leadership role in a way that is functional to the project. This kind of team maturity means that the team can assume most if not all of the responsibilities of a self-managed work team. This does not mean that project leaders can ignore the project team or abdicate their leadership role. Project work is monitored, of course, so that no surprises will occur. It does mean, however, that project leaders can turn more of their attention to other matters vital to the project, such as liaisoning, planning, forecasting problems, and adapting to change.

Adjourning

All project work ends, and project members may leave earlier than project completion if their contributions are complete. Adjourning is a process that should command the project leader's attention as well. The contributions of project members should be recognized so that project members can feel good about their work. Debriefs or after-action reviews should also be conducted, either formally or informally, to wrap up the lessons learned from the project.

Wise project leaders will also take note of those members who were particularly valuable to the project and who went above and beyond the call of duty. Special rewards and thanks should be given to them. Word gets around about leaders who reward good work—and those who ignore it. Leaders should also keep track of particularly good personnel for the next project that may need their skills.

Summary

The term *team* has been used to refer to many different kinds of groups. In this chapter, we use Katzenbach and Smith's characterization.[16] A team is a small number of people with complementary skills who are committed to a common purpose, a common set of performance goals, and a common approach for which they hold themselves mutually accountable.

There are at least three criteria to assess team success. First and foremost, successful teams deliver the goods to their clients—on time, on budget, and according to specification. Project leaders need to be aware, however, that many stakeholders are involved in determining project success, and their views need attention as well. Second, successful teams also get better at what they do—they develop into better teams and team members. Attention to team development pays off even when dealing with temporary project teams. Finally, successful teams are committed to the project, to one another, and to their leader.

Teams have a number of characteristics that should be considered when building, developing, and leading them. The first is team size. Smaller teams tend to do better than larger teams. Larger teams suffer process losses and tend to break down into smaller groups. A second consideration is the knowledge, skills, and abilities of those who compose the team. Skills to do the task work, skills needed to attend to people issues, and managerial and leadership skills are all needed in project work. A third important issue is team governance. Although project teams may start out as manager-led teams, more productive teams evolve into self-managed work teams with autonomy and control over their own operations as they pursue project objectives. A fourth factor to consider is that teams need an identity of their own. They need to have definite boundaries and to be seen as a team both by themselves and by others. A fifth issue to consider is how the team will interact with one another. Digital communications can offer a great deal to project work. Face-to-face interactions, however, provide the richest form of communication and provide the team with more power over its members. Face-to-face interactions are particularly helpful at crucial junctures of a project like at its initiation, at important milestones, and when confronting important problems. A final consideration is that teams need to develop a common ideology—common ideas and a common understanding of the team, its norms, its roles, and its goals. Successful teams often use a few pivotal norms to hold themselves accountable to one another and to the project. Members of successful project teams also perform their roles well. Common problems that undermine good role performance include not enacting important roles that need to be played, different team members' having different expectations of a person's role, and not having the knowledge, skills, or abilities to play one's role well. The goals of successful teams are also understood and shared by everyone on the team. One way to develop a common understanding of team norms, roles, and goals is to openly discuss them early in a project and to view their discussion as legitimate throughout the project as the need arises.

Teams develop through different stages—forming, storming, norming, performing, and adjourning. The forming stage is characterized by polite restraint on the part of team members who may be strangers to one another. At this stage, the team is uncertain about the goals of the team and the roles they will play in it. They are also unsure about how the team will be led. These and similar issues of concern need to be addressed early in a project. Although project leaders may witness a fair amount of silent affirmation of their leadership at this early stage of development, they should be aware that this may be due to team members' simply holding back comments, which is characteristic of this stage.

The storming stage is characterized by open or covert conflict over project issues. This stage emerges because different people have different ideas about the project. Project leaders should not be surprised or angry when such differences arise. Some ideas might be used to make the project better and, in any event, differences are more productively addressed early rather than later in the project cycle. Most team members want project differences resolved and look to the project leader to do so. They will tend to defer to the leader if they believe that their views are given due consideration.

The norming stage is when the project team has come to understand, accept, and commit to the norms, roles, and goals of a project. Noticeable characteristics are team cohesion and commitment to the project. The performing stage is when the project team functions as a team performing project work in a well-coordinated fashion, making effective and productive decisions, and dealing with team issues well as they arise. As teams move through the norming and performing stages, they can assume more and more of the responsibilities of a self-managed work team, allowing project leaders to spend more time on their other leadership responsibilities.

Adjourning is the stage when the project ends. This is the time for looking back and taking stock of the project—to take note and record important lessons learned. Project leaders do well to recognize good performance and keep track of productive project personnel for future projects.

Review Questions

1. How does the chapter define a team?
    a. How do the components relate to team effectiveness?
2. Identify and discuss the criteria for team success.
    a. Give a concrete example of each one in terms of a project.
3. Six factors were identified as fundamentals of team structure that play key roles in the building, development, and leading of teams.
    a. Identify and discuss the effects of each factor.
    b. With regard to ideology, discuss the effects of team norms, roles, and goals and some of the problems encountered with each of them. With each, present how a project leader might address those problems.
4. Identify and characterize the stages of development a team goes through from first coming together to full maturity.
    a. What, if any, are the needs that leaders should address at each stage of development?

Exercises

1. Identify one or two of the best and one or two of the worst school or work teams on which you served as a member.
    a. Identify the top three to five factors that made the team the best or the worst in terms of your experience.
    b. To what extent do those factors coincide with issues covered in this chapter?
    c. How do the factors you have identified add to the issues covered?
    d. If you were the leader of the worst teams with full authority over them, what would be the top 10 things you would do to ensure their success?
2. Using the best and worst teams identified previously, develop a profile of each team using the table "Comparison Issues for Best and Worst Teams."
    a. Use the criteria of team success in your profile.
    b. Review the fundamentals of team structure in your profile.
    c. Review the stages of team development and consider the extent to which the team matured and the stages through which it progressed. What needs at each stage were addressed or ignored? What was the effect?

Table 5.1   Comparison Issues for Best and Worst Teams

	Best	Best	Worst	Worst
Success Criteria				
Goal accomplishment				
Development				
Satisfaction				
Team Structure				
Team size				
Composition				
Governance				
Interactions				
Team norms				
Team roles				
Team goals				
Team Development				
Forming				
Storming				
Norming				
Performing				
Adjourning				

3. You have just been made leader of a project of your own choosing.
   a. Think through and describe the project.
   b. Present what you would do to help pull together, develop, and lead your team. Pay particular attention to team and project needs in the early stages of team development and how you would respond to them.

4. If you are a member of a class team, discuss its norms, roles, and goals. Use this chapter as a starting point for your discussion. Work toward common agreement about a few pivotal norms with which all can agree, important roles and how and who should play them, and the concrete deliverables your team will produce.

Endnotes

1. Katzenbach, J. R., & Smith, D. K. (1993, March/April). The discipline of teams. *Harvard Business Review, 71,* 111–120.

2. (1993).

3. Hackman, J. R. (2002). *Leading teams: Setting the stage for great performances.* Boston: Harvard Business School Press. Goodman, D. S., Ravlin, E., & Schminke, M. (1987). Understanding groups in organizations. In L. L. Cummings & B. Staw (Eds.), *Research in organizational behavior* (Vol. 9, pp. 121–173). Greenwich, CT: JAI.

4. I am aware of many project leaders who have the reputation of being "hard drivers" but who have no difficulty recruiting willing project members because members know that the leader attends to their development as well as to the project's deliverables.

5. Steiner, I. D. (1972). *Group process and productivity.* New York: Academic Press.

6. I know of a number of project leaders who have made serious mistakes in this regard. One, for example, made the decision to transfer a particularly bothersome team member offsite to serve as liaison to the client just to get rid of him. Needless to say, this turned out to be a serious error.

7. These governance examples are from: Hackman, J. R. (1987). The design of work teams. In J. W. Lorsch (Ed.), *Handbook of organizational behavior* (pp. 315–342). Upper Saddle River, NJ: Prentice Hall.

8. Hackman (2002).

9. Cascio, W. (2000). Managing a virtual workplace. *Academy of Management Executive, 14*(2), 81–90. Townsend, A. M., DeMarie, S. M., & Hendricson, A. R. (1998). Virtual teams: Technology and the workplace of the future. *Academy of Management Executive, 12*(3), 17–29.

10. The notion of a "group mind" has received more attention in recent years. See, for example: Austin, J. (2003). Transactive memory in organizational groups: The effects of content, consensus, specialization, and accuracy on group performance. *Journal of Applied Psychology, 88,* 866–878. Gibson, C. (2001). From knowledge accumulation to accommodation: Cycles of collective cognition in work groups. *Journal of Organizational Behavior, 22,* 121–134. Marks, M. A., Burke, C. S., Sabella, M. J., & Zaccaro, S. J. (2002). The impact of cross-training on team effectiveness. *Journal of Applied Psychology, 87,* 3–13.

11. Hackman (2002).

12. More experienced project personnel take far less time to do so than those new to project work.

13. The following discussion is based on: Tuckman, B. W., & Jensen, M.A.C. (1977). Stages of small group development revisited. *Group and Organization Studies, 2,* 419–428. This discussion also includes information from: Obert, S. L. (1978). *The development of organizational task groups.* Ph.D. dissertation, Case Western Reserve University, as cited in: Cohen, A. R., Fink, S. L., Gadon, H., & Willits, R. D. (1984). *Effective behavior in organizations.* Homewood, IL: Irwin.

14. Leaders need to carefully consider the longer term consequences of ideas brought to them. Project members quite often do not have the broader project picture held by the project leader. Leaders need to take on changes very carefully with full consideration given to effects on the project schedule, budget, and deliverables as well as on relevant stakeholders.

15. Although not common, some project members may continue to engage in destructive and disruptive conflict for reasons of their own. The project leader should seek to solidify the rest of the project team in the face of such opposition then move to remove it if it cannot be constructively resolved.

16. (1993).

6

The Project Team's Environment

Introduction	102
The Achievement Project	102
Overview of Chapter	102
Stakeholders	103
Project Clients	103
Host Management	105
The Project Team	105
External Suppliers	106
Internal Suppliers	106
Regulators	107
End Users and Implementers	108
Political Players	108
Developing and Using Project Networks	109
The Nature of Social Capital	110
Developing Social Capital	113
Summary	114
Review Questions	116
Exercises	117
Endnotes	117
Figure 6.1: The Social Network of Leanne Phillips's Principal Project Team	110

Figure 6.2: The Social Network of the Achievement
    Project Organization   111
Figure 6.3: The Social Network of the Achievement Project
    Organization and Its Larger Stakeholder Network   112

Introduction

The Achievement Project

In Chapter 5, we met Leanne Phillips. She works for the Los Padres School District and was charged by the board of supervisors to lead an important project. Changes in federal regulations threatened the funding received by the district. A small but sizable percentage of students were not meeting the achievement levels mandated by the regulations. The board charged Leanne with identifying the most critical issues involved in the problem, developing the information they would need to understand and address those issues, and making recommendations about courses of action the board should take.

It wasn't long before word got out about the project. In fact, the "Achievement Project" was the name the local newspaper gave it, and the local TV and radio news programs picked it up. In a matter of just two days, Leanne was receiving dozens of calls and more than 30 e-mails each day from people who were interested—and wanted to have a say—in the Achievement Project. Teachers, principals, board members, and the presidents of various parent-teacher association chapters in the district were all calling her. So, too, were salespeople with a wide variety of products for at-risk students. The legal counsel for the district was also in touch with her, as were regulators from the state's department of education. Leanne Phillips was only three days into the project, and she knew there would be many others out there who would have an interest in the project.

Overview of Chapter

Leanne Phillips is receiving a much larger dose of what most project leaders receive in their projects. Projects never exist in isolation. They are always connected to a network of people and organizations—stakeholders— who are affected by them in some way and who want to influence them. Project leaders need to be able to identify these important stakeholders and manage their interactions with the project.

This chapter focuses on project stakeholders and how to work with them. We first examine different kinds of stakeholders, some of the key things they desire, and how project leaders might respond to them. We then turn our attention to look at the project environment more strategically. Project leaders play a critical role in managing the external networks of their project's stakeholders. What those networks look like, the role project leaders need to play in them, and how to develop and maintain those networks are addressed.

Stakeholders

Stakeholders are those people, organizational units, and institutions that have a stake in the conduct and outcome of the project. Stakeholders become more critical to the project the more they are affected by the project and the more they have a say in affecting its conduct and outcomes. Balancing the interests, desires, and needs of so diverse a group is a challenge for any project leader.

Each project will have its own unique profile of stakeholders, but we will examine some of the more common ones in this section. We look first at three particularly important stakeholders: project clients, the managers of the organization that hosts the project, and the project team. For various reasons, these stakeholders usually have a great deal of say in how a project is set up and conducted. We then examine external and internal resource suppliers. Projects depend on others for resources and so they, too, have a stake in the project. We give attention next to regulators. Projects often have to meet regulatory standards, so leaders need to work with those who enforce them. Many projects are intended to benefit others who will come after the project is done. These postproject end users of the project need to be addressed as well as any "implementers" who may be tasked with implementing any project recommendations to help them. Finally, we address a set of stakeholders who are often ignored in the project management literature but who are important nonetheless: political players—the informal champions and opponents with whom projects often deal.

Project Clients

Project clients are those who sponsor or fund the project. The reason why clients sponsor a project at all is because they want it to address some set of their needs. Project leaders usually work with clients throughout the project but their services often differ at the beginning of, during, and at the closing of projects.

At the beginning of projects, leaders must often help clients clarify their needs in terms of project objectives and concrete deliverables. Chapter 2 is largely dedicated to this all-important activity, but one key point is worth repeating. Clients often have only vague ideas about their needs and how a project might address them in terms of concrete products and services. Helping clients to move through this identification process is one of the most important services project leaders can provide their clients and their own project teams. The process of determining specific project deliverables can occur quickly and easily or, as is likely in Leanne Phillips's case, it can take quite some effort. It is critical, however, that a project charter—with deliverables, budget, and a timeline spelled out—be developed and agreed to by the client, the host organization, and the project leader.

During the course of the project, clients will often want assurances that the project is proceeding as planned. This need is generally best met by structuring milestones into the project at which progress is noted, formal reports are made, and important issues are discussed. These reporting events require effort, resources, and time and should be included in the project's planning and budgeting as such. This is not to say, however, that client contact can or should be strictly limited to these events. Some clients can be rather high maintenance, and, in any event, project leaders will want to keep their clients appropriately informed about important developments. Every effort should be made, however, to buffer the project team from undue disturbances in their work.

The close of a project is signaled by the delivery of the project's final products and services. Many project leaders develop and work through "punch cards" or check-off lists with clients in the actual delivery of products and services. Tied to the initial specification of project deliverables, these can be useful tools for focusing attention on key closing elements. Often, postdelivery work may be required to fully close down a project and satisfy a client. Project leaders need to be aware of this and incorporate postdelivery work into the project plan and budget.

The project's aim is to meet or exceed the client's expectations. The key concept, here, is expectations. From the initial specification of project deliverables to the project's conclusion, the leader needs to keep track of and manage those expectations. During the course of a project, for example, clients may get other ideas for products and services they would like. Project leaders will generally want to work with clients to show how such changes—known as "scope creep"—will require additional time and resources and refocus their attention on the originally agreed-on deliverables. Often changes can be discussed in terms of follow-on projects.

Working with clients can be a challenge. Many project leaders feel uncomfortable meeting and establishing working relationships with new people. Nevertheless, the client plays too many critical roles in the project to be ignored.

Host Management

Upper management in the host organization is also a significant stakeholder. The project leader's direct supervisor is one of the most significant of those. In project and matrix organizations, projects are undertaken as the company's business. In such cases, higher management's aims are that projects remain profitable and be conducted within the operating budget and other constraints established for project work.

Often, as in the case of the Achievement Project, projects are undertaken for the benefit of the organization itself. In these cases, higher management also plays the role of an outside client and can pose the same kinds of challenges presented by them.

In all cases, project leaders will want their direct supervisors and higher management to support and champion the projects they lead: to help make sure that the project gets the resources it needs and run interference for the project as it progresses though its life cycle.

For its part, management wants to know that the project is proceeding as planned. Structured progress reports similar to those given to clients can serve this need.[1] Unexpected problems of strategic importance need to be brought to management's attention quickly along with options to address the problems. Higher management, however, generally expects project leaders to handle routine project problems of a more tactical nature in the context of the project itself.

The Project Team

Projects are unique endeavors and require a great deal of problem solving to produce the products or services required. Most often, projects work under strict timelines and budgets. In addition, project personnel often have organizational commitments other than the project itself. All of these characteristics can combine to produce a fair amount of stress on project teams.

Project teams want to be able to do the project—to bring it to a successful conclusion. Initially, teams want to clearly understand the project and how it is to be done. Toward these ends, leaders need to present the team with clear project objectives and a clear, actionable plan to achieve them. The team also needs the resources required for the project. The most important of these is the composition of the team itself. The members need to possess the knowledge, skills, and abilities required by the project. During the conduct of the project, resources need to arrive according to specifications and when needed.[2]

As project teams conduct the project, they need to be protected from unnecessary outside pressures that will distract them. Projects have many stakeholders with varied interests, and project leaders need to buffer their teams while leaders themselves develop the stakeholder linkages appropriate to the team's work.

Finally, project members do not want to be overcommitted. Project leaders need to be aware of and sensitive to the demands placed on members of their team. In addition to careful scheduling, leaders should work with those outside the project who have a legitimate claim on project personnel to help clear their schedules.

External Suppliers

External suppliers are those outside the organization who provide project resources. These resources are often critical to project success and need to arrive on time, as budgeted, and according to specifications. It is not uncommon to find, however, that external suppliers are less motivated by these needs than the project leader. Contrary to popular belief, just because something is paid for doesn't mean that the project will get what it needs when planned.

Contractual arrangements should be developed for the delivery of critical and unique resources. Even so, with these and all other important resources, leaders should schedule lead times to attend to their delivery. It is a good idea, too, for project leaders to establish relationships with their critical vendors. If at all possible, leaders should get to know at least one contact person who can pull strings with their vendors.

Internal Suppliers

Internal suppliers are those in the host organization who supply the project with resources. Personnel and information are the most common resources provided, but things like office space, the loan of equipment, and even raw material might be provided.

Even in project organizations in which functional managers are expected to provide project personnel, conflicts emerge over who gets assigned, when, and for how long. In more traditional organizations in which others are imposed on to provide help to a project, the conflict potential is even higher. Providing resources to others often produces problems of scheduling, conflicts between requests from other projects, and the day-to-day demands pressing on the supplier's own unit. Project leaders need to be as sensitive as possible to these issues.

It is important for project leaders to work as closely as they can with the suppliers they need. They should strive to give as much lead time as possible so supplying units can work around the loss. If resources are needed on a continuing basis, developing a more personal relationship can help. In all cases, gratitude for the help provided is appreciated.

If, despite all good efforts, resources are still not forthcoming, project leaders might well have to take alternative actions. As a last resort, higher management can be asked to address the resource problem. Higher management generally prefers to have these matters taken care of by their subordinates. Using higher management tends to expend political capital and rarely wins friends from the supplying unit.

Regulators

Projects often have to pass certain levels of quality in their products and services or in the way the project itself is conducted. Making sure those levels of quality are met is the aim of regulators.

Outside regulators are usually independent organizations or agencies formally mandated to check up on project deliverables or the conduct of projects. Building inspectors, for example, check up on the structural regulations of construction. Inspectors from the Occupational Safety and Health Administration make sure the physical welfare of project workers is being addressed. Internal regulators work for the host organization and generally attend to the conduct of the project (e.g., internal auditors and the contracts office). State, federal, and district regulators will play these outside and internal regulatory roles in Leanne Phillips's project.

To be truly effective, regulators must be independent of the project and its organizational line of authority. Moreover, regulators are often required to limit their interactions with those whom they regulate to maintain their objectivity. When regulators find that project work is out of compliance, for example, they may have the authority to shut down a project yet not be allowed to suggest remedial changes. All these aspects of the regulatory relationship make working with regulators something of a challenge.[3]

Meticulous care must be given to regulatory requirements in the planning, budgeting, and conduct of any project. As the costs of regulatory failure rise in a project, leaders might well consider early, preliminary inspections or the use of outside consultants with regulatory experience to review the project and its conduct as needed.

End Users and Implementers

Projects are often designed to benefit others besides the sponsoring client. Leanne Phillips's project is only one example. The ultimate end users of her project are the at-risk students with low achievement scores. Like many projects, Leanne's project will end before these ultimate users will make use of her work. Although the project's recommendations will hopefully benefit these students, the Achievement Project itself will not implement the recommendations. Even so, such projects should be planned and executed with these stakeholders in mind.[4]

Other postproject stakeholders are those who will implement the project's recommendations. For a variety of obvious reasons, the project team is often well suited to implement the products and services they have produced. Clients frequently require initial implementation as part of the project with a period of product and service maintenance thereafter. Other projects, however, recommend postproject actions and rely on others to implement them. In the Achievement Project, for example, the teachers of the at-risk students and the principals of the schools they attend will play implementing roles for those recommendations approved by the board. Although Leanne Phillips's team may not implement the project's recommendations, the more they know of the challenges faced by those who will and the resources they will need, the better, more action oriented their recommendations can be. Project leaders need to plan for and have their projects funded to produce these kinds of objectives.[5]

Political Players

Finally, the project leader needs to be aware of another kind of stakeholder: political players. It has long been known that once you step into a leadership role, you are also stepping into a political arena.[6] Projects in particular can kick up "political dust." Projects are designed to make things happen, to bring things into being that were not there before. This means change—change caused by the simple conduct of the project as well as the change envisioned by the completion of the project. Any change will have supporters and opponents. Rarely mentioned in the project management literature are the political stakeholders who are likely to emerge with the conduct of almost any project.

Project supporters and opponents can often be identified by asking a simple question: "Who will benefit and who will lose by the conduct and completion of this project?" The recommendations made by the Achievement Project, for example, may well benefit some in the school district's organization and cause loss to others. The same might be true of some constituencies external to the district's organization. These will form part of the possible pool of political supporters and opponents of the project.

Some opponents are not opposed to the outcomes of the project as such, but to its imposition on their operations. Although an organizational unit in the organization may be ordered to help the project in some aspect of its work, for example, those in the unit may actively resist that aid for any of a number of reasons.

Unfortunately, organizational politics may also play a role in the larger context of a project. The success or failure of a project may affect the political fortunes of not only its leader but also others in the organization. The extent to which a project is successful, for example, may mean that its leader will rise in the organization while others do not.

Although projects have their opponents, so, too, do they have their supporters. Clients and those in upper management should be major supporters. The project leader's direct supervisor should be one of the project's key champions. Keeping one's supervisors up to date on the project's progress and demonstrating one's ability to handle the problems that always arise will help keep the support one needs. There are likely other supporters of a project as well. As a general practice, it pays to stop by to let them know how things are going. Project leaders sometimes have a tendency to call on their supporters only when they need them. It is also a good idea to call on them when things are going well and take the opportunity to thank them for their continuing support.

It is always a good idea to give some thought to the political side of a project. If its political potential is high—as it is with the Achievement Project—identifying and reaching out to supporters as early as possible is a good idea. Their thoughts on the political side of the project can help leaders in the planning and conduct of a politically sensitive project. Establishing relationships early with supporters, identifying likely detractors, and planning when support will be needed is an unfortunate but often necessary side of successful project leadership.

Developing and Using Project Networks

The previous section makes clear that projects never exist in isolation. They are surrounded by many stakeholders who will affect the conduct of the project and determine its success or failure. Being able to work in this larger network of stakeholders is one of the more important assets leaders can bring to their projects.[7] That asset has come to be called *social capital*.[8] In this section, we examine first what social capital is and then address how leaders can develop social capital in project work.

The Nature of Social Capital

The term *capital* is used by economists to refer to any asset that can be employed to produce wealth. Buildings and equipment used to manufacture products, for example, are capital assets. Human capital is composed of the knowledge, skills, and abilities of a person that can be used to produce things of value such as deliverables from project tasks. Social capital comes from a person's connections to others. It is the value someone has because he or she can tap into various social networks to get the resources needed for a job or to help coordinate, assist, or run interference for a project. A project leader's social capital, then, is his or her ability to use the resources of others in the furtherance of project work.

We all know others we can turn to when we are in need of help and, in turn, we often provide our help to others. That is what social capital really is all about. Some project leaders, however, have far more social capital, and more project-relevant social capital than others. Consider, for example, Figures 6.1, 6.2, and 6.3.[9] All these figures show graphical representations

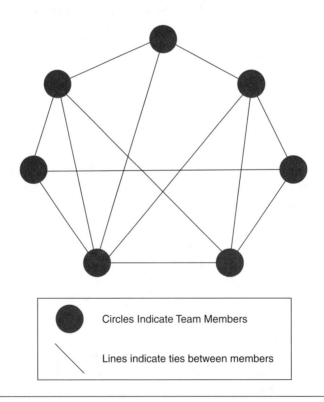

Figure 6.1   The Social Network of Leanne Phillips's Principal Project Team

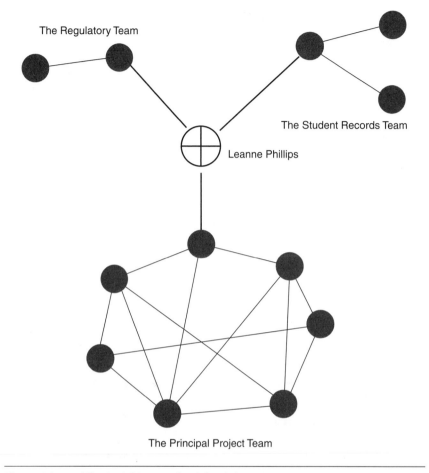

The Regulatory Team

The Student Records Team

Leanne Phillips

The Principal Project Team

Figure 6.2   The Social Network of the Achievement Project Organization

of different social networks in the Achievement Project. Figure 6.1 shows the social network of Leanne Phillips's principal seven-member project team. This team does the heavy lifting for the project and is responsible for most project work. In the graph, each circle represents a team member and each line a tie that binds one member to another. This team appears to be a very cohesive one. Each member is tied to all the other members and, no doubt, can turn to them for help.

Figure 6.2 represents the social network of the larger Achievement Project organization. In addition to the principal project team, there are two others. One two-person team works on regulatory issues as needed. The other three-member team works on reviewing the records of at-risk students in the district. The student records team does not appear to be as

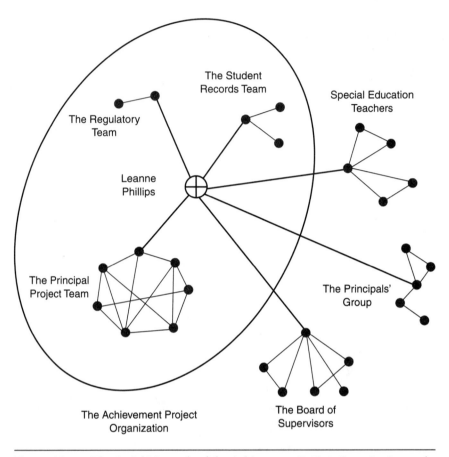

The Student
Records Team

Special Education
Teachers

The Regulatory
Team

Leanne
Phillips

The Principal
Project Team

The Principals'
Group

The Achievement Project
Organization

The Board of
Supervisors

Figure 6.3   The Social Network of the Achievement Project Organization and
Its Larger Stakeholder Network

cohesive as the principal project team because two of its members are not
tied very well to one another, although both are tied to what appears to be
a formal or informal team leader. Leanne Phillips has ties to all the teams.
In the social network of the Achievement Project, then, Leanne Phillips has
the most social capital. She can call on all the project teams for project
work and support, whereas members of each team can call only on themselves. Leanne Phillips's position in this kind of social network is what one
would expect of a project leader.

Figure 6.3 shows the Achievement Project organization in relation to
some of its key stakeholders in its larger environment. One key stakeholder,
of course, is the board of supervisors. Leanne Phillips reports to them, and

they depend on her to lead the Achievement Project organization. Two other stakeholder groups are the special education teachers and the principals' group. The special education teachers will have to implement and carry through some of the recommendations of the Achievement Project. The school principals will be responsible for overseeing the implementation of those recommendations and for the students' achievements, and they will need to report to the board about the progress of the Achievement Program.

A few things are important to note in Figure 6.3. First, Leanne Phillips is tied to all stakeholder groups. This means she has some measure of access to these stakeholder groups, and, to the extent she can enlist their aid and support, she has social capital because of those ties. Second, although the members of the various stakeholder groups are not closely tied to one another, at least one member in each is tied to all the rest. That fact makes the member relatively more influential in that stakeholder group. Finally, Leanne Phillips's ties to each group are through its more influential member. That provides her with more social capital than if her ties were with less influential members.

Although some of a project leader's ties to others in this extended network may be very strong, many may be weak but quite serviceable ties. Strong ties come from constant interaction, day in and day out, over a whole host of issues important to a relationship. These kinds of ties make up strong teams. Weak ties are more like working relationships. Hopefully friendly, they tend to center on the exchange of resources each member of the network seeks from the other. As these relationships become stronger, the parties become more committed to them. Project success is based a great deal on the social capital of project members. Most often, this centers on the social capital of project leaders based on their position in the larger project network and their ability to use the ties they have developed.

Developing Social Capital

Social capital is produced by developing relationships with people who have the resources and influence needed for project success. In the early project planning stage, leaders need to identify all those stakeholders who will play important decisionmaking and resource sharing roles for the project. Once identified, project leaders need to self-consciously set up plans to talk at length with these stakeholders about the project.

Initial interactions are best done face-to-face and one-on-one. These kinds of one-on-one meetings allow for more candid conversations and richer communication. The project leader's agenda includes assessing the stakeholder's interests in the project, his or her likely influence over the project, and the true role he or she will seek to play in it. Active listening is a key skill to employ in these meetings. A great deal can be learned, for example, by taking note of the questions stakeholders ask. Their questions reveal their interests, and attention to nonverbal communication can reveal the intensity of those interests. Their knowledge of other stakeholders can reveal their ties to them and, often, the influence of other stakeholders in the project's larger network.

As the project progresses, project leaders need to spend time working with the more influential stakeholders and those who have access to important project resources. These meetings can happen in formal venues like project meetings or less formal venues like luncheons.

Many project leaders shy away from these kinds of networking tasks. Often coming from a more technical background, they prefer to work on the project itself rather than on the networks that surround the project. Successful leaders, however, spend much of their time on such networking tasks. The social capital provided by project networks provides project leaders with the information, support, and other resources that they need to be successful. Project leaders should not think of networking work as taking them away from project work. Rather, networking *is* the kind of project work required of them.

Summary

Projects never exist in isolation. They are surrounded by a network of stakeholders, often with different interests in the project, who can determine its success or failure. In this chapter, we examined various stakeholders, their interests, and how project leaders might respond to them. We went on to examine the networks to which stakeholders belong and the role of the project leader in developing and working with those networks.

Stakeholders are those who have an interest or stake in the conduct or outcomes of a project. We examined eight kinds of stakeholders in this chapter. Project clients are those who sponsor or fund a project. They are interested in the project because it is supposed to address some set of their needs. At the beginning of a project, leaders often need to help clients clarify their needs and how they might be addressed by concrete project deliverables. This is one of the most valuable services project leaders can provide to their clients as well as to the future project team. During the course of the project, clients often like to be kept informed of its progress. This is best done with structured progress reports and with additional communications as required. The transferal of final project deliverables signals the conclusion of the project. Project leaders want to meet or exceed client expectations with those deliverables and need to manage those expectations from the beginning to the end of the project. Project leaders often find checklists a useful tool to focus attention on the key deliverables of a project. Often, postdelivery work must be done to fully close the project and satisfy the client. The time and costs of postdelivery work should be incorporated into project plans.

Managers in the host organization are also important stakeholders, and one's direct supervisor is key among them. Host managers want the project to proceed as planned, and project leaders want host managers to support and champion their projects. Providing structured progress reports to management, keeping management informed of strategic issues and problems, and handling tactical problems in the project itself will generally conform to management expectations.

The project team is an important stakeholder as well. The team members want to know that they can bring the project to a successful conclusion. At the beginning of a project, the team wants the leader to provide clear project objectives and action plans. The members want the leader to provide the necessary resources to do the project when they are needed and to buffer the project team from unnecessary outside pressures. Project members often have commitments other than the project itself, and they would like the leader to plan for those commitments as well.

External suppliers or vendors are another class of stakeholder. They provide often critical and unique resources to the project, and the scheduled delivery of those resources according to specification is important to project success. Project leaders are well advised to check on the delivery of resources prior to their scheduled transfer and to develop deeper relationships with more critical vendors.

Internal suppliers are those in the host organization who supply the project with resources such as personnel and information. Even when the provision of resources is expected and planned, those providing resources may see their provision as an imposition. Project leaders need to be sensitive to these issues and work with the supplying unit as closely as possible. Although problems with internal supply might have to be taken to higher-level management, they are best resolved at lower levels.

Regulators have a stake in the quality of the conduct or output of a project. Their aim is to certify conformance to regulatory standards. Meticulous care should be given to regulatory requirements in the planning, budgeting, and conduct of the project. In some cases, the use of outside experts to review the project or its output can help address certification needs.

End users and implementers are postproject stakeholders. Projects are often designed to benefit users other than sponsoring clients themselves. Postproject users should be addressed in the planning and budgeting of the project in consultation with the client. Implementers are those who will implement the project's recommendations. Although projects most often implement the products and services they produce, many do not. In those cases, the more the project team knows of the challenges implementers will face, the more action oriented and useful their recommendations can be. Materials and resources are often uncovered during the course of a project that can be useful to implementers. Simply cataloging those resources is a low-cost, value-added component project leaders should consider providing.

Finally, projects have political stakeholders. Projects are designed to change things. Changes create benefits and losses for those affected by them. Those who see a loss because of the conduct or outcome of a project can be expected to oppose it. Those who see benefits are likely to be supporters. Unfortunately, project success itself may also threaten those who see themselves in competition with the project leader for promotions and the like. It is a good idea, then, for project leaders to think through the political aspects of their projects as well as the technical ones.

Projects and their stakeholders are tied together into project networks. Being able to work well in these networks is an important role for project leaders. A key asset in doing so is social capital. Social capital comes from one's relationships with others who can provide help to a project. Although many project leaders would prefer to concentrate on ties with the primary project team, the success of their projects requires them to develop ties to the broader array of stakeholders in a project's larger network. Many if not most of these ties are not strong. They are the weaker kind of ties expected in resource-sharing business arrangements—friendly but business related. Relationships with other individuals more critical to the project and to the leader's career should be cultivated so that stronger ties to them can be developed.

Social capital in a project is developed early in the planning phase of a project. Stakeholders are identified and initial contacts are made. These contacts are best made face to face and one on one if possible to facilitate better communications. As the project progresses, the leader needs to spend more time with the more influential stakeholders of the project. Although many project leaders shy away from this kind of networking, they need to understand that this kind of activity is a critical part of the project leadership role.

Review Questions

1. What is a project stakeholder?

2. Compare and contrast the interests of project clients and higher management in the host organization.

3. What are the similarities and differences between external and internal suppliers?
    a. How should a project leader attend to each?

4. What are the roles political stakeholders can play in a project?
    a. What are the factors that affect whether political stakeholders will emerge?

5. What is meant by social capital?
    a. What role do strong ties and weak links play in social capital?

6. Why do some project leaders have more social capital than others?

7. How does a project leader go about developing his or her social capital?

Exercises

1. You are a project leader of a project to increase the efficiency of loading and unloading material from your company's dock.
    a. Who are the likely stakeholders in your project?
    b. How should you address their interests?

2. You are the leader of a project to set up a new store for your company. The company wants to open up 100 of these stores nationwide in the next year. The project entails finding a suitable location in a specific geographic area designated by the company and developing a turnkey operation—one that is ready for immediate use.
    a. Who are the likely stakeholders in your project?
    b. How should you address their interests?

3. Take a quick inventory of your social capital. Do so by first identifying the strong social ties you have to others in your organization (you can use your college as an organization if you are a student). Next, identify your weak links to important and influential people in your organization. Is the profile of your social capital more like Figure 6.1, 6.2, or 6.3?

4. You have just been put in charge of an important project in your organization that will affect a number of operations directly and indirectly.
    a. Define this project in any way you wish.
    b. Discuss how you would go about developing your social capital on this project. Be as specific as you can.

Endnotes

1. Managers tend to have preferences about the nature or kind of reports they like (e.g., verbal or written, extensive or summary), the timing of them, and the contents of reports (e.g., covering only problems that have arisen or furnishing more detail about current budget use, progress). It is an important aspect of project

leadership, then, to know your supervisor's preferences and meet them to his or her satisfaction.

2. I recall a story about a Canadian high-rise construction firm that consistently came in on budget and on schedule in all its projects—an almost unheard of success story. It turned out that one of its secrets was that it made sure workers it got the materials they needed when they needed them. Having project resources available when project members need them is a vital part of project success.

3. Sometimes, closer working relationships develop between project leaders and some of the regulators who oversee their work. If that is the case, it is important not to abuse the relationship. Project leaders need to work with the regulator to meet the standards required, not to bypass them.

4. The Project Management Institute clearly defines customers as end users. Some projects are designed primarily for the end user or customer. For example, new medicines are designed for the end user even though the costs of research and development are borne by the sponsoring clients. Project success, then, depends on how the end user benefits. Project leaders, then, should keep an interest in the end user. Sponsoring clients often have their interests in mind. Clients may also rehire project teams or their host organizations to follow up on and carry out their own recommendations or some part of them for the end user. A project's clear commitment to users will increase this likelihood.

5. Often, project teams come across resources and material that may be useful to implementers. Collecting or cataloging these kinds of resources can be a low-cost, high value-added addition to a project.

6. Kakabadse, A., & Parker, C. (Eds.). (1984). *Power, politics, and organizations: A behavioral science view.* New York: John Wiley and Sons. Pfeffer, J. (1981). *Power in organizations.* Marshfield, MA: Pitman. Mintzberg, H. (1983). *Power in and around organizations.* Englewood Cliffs, NJ: Prentice-Hall.

7. Ancona, D. G., & Caldwell, D. (1992). Bridging the boundary: External activity and performance in organizational teams. *Administrative Science Quarterly, 37,* 634–665.

8. Coleman, J. (1988). Social capital in the creation of human capital. *American Journal of Sociology, 94,* 95–120. See also Leana, C. R., & Van Buren, H. J., III. (1999). Organizational social capital and employment practices. *Academy of Management Review, 24,* 538–556.

9. Burt, R. S. (1992). *The social structure of competition.* Cambridge, MA: Harvard University Press. Burt, R. S. (1999). Entrepreneurs, distrust, and third parties: A strategic look at the dark side of defense works. In L. Thompson, J. Levine, & D. Messick (Eds.), *Shared cognition in organizations: The management of knowledge* (pp. 213–243). Mahway, NJ: Laurence Erlbaum. Adapted by Thompson, L. L. (2004), *Making the team: A guide for managers* (2nd ed.). Upper Saddle River, NJ: Prentice Hall.

7

Leading Project Teams

Introduction	120
John's Promotion	120
Chapter Overview	120
The Roles of a Project Leader	121
External Role Requirements	121
Figurehead and Spokesperson	121
Liaison and Monitor	122
Champion and Negotiator	122
Controller	123
Internal Role Requirements	123
Planner and Resource Allocator	123
Coordinator	124
Problem Solver	124
Team Leader	124
Clarifying the Leadership Role	125
Project Leadership and the Project's Life Cycle	126
The Early Stages: Initiation and Planning	126
Project Launch	127
Project Execution	129
The Project Team	129
External Stakeholders	131
Project Closing	132
Project Leadership and Individual Project Members	133

Summary	134
Review Questions	138
Exercises	138
Endnotes	138

Introduction

John's Promotion

John Billings was looking at his boss, Mark White, with feelings of both admiration and a kind of creeping apprehension. John's boss had been promoted to department head in SPUR, a division of APEX, a large government-contracting firm. When Mark received his promotion, he recommended John to fill his position: one of three section leaders who report to the department head. John jumped at the opportunity and soon would receive a hefty increase in salary along with his promotion.

Mark White was laying out the various accounts John would be taking over when his feelings of admiration and apprehension began to emerge. Two accounts were still in the negotiation stage, one was ready to launch, and three more were continuing projects but one of those was scheduled for closing at the end of the month.

John knew everyone in the section, of course, but now he would be dealing with them in a whole new relationship as section manager. In addition, he would be dealing much more closely with higher management, clients, and others outside the department in his new position.

John's feelings of admiration focused on Mark. He really was a good leader and deserved his promotion. His boots would be hard to fill, and that began to lead to John's feelings of apprehension. Despite working on projects in the section for some time now, John began to realize that he had only the smallest notion of what he would have to do to be successful in his new role as a manager leading so many projects.

Chapter Overview

John's concerns are widely shared by those new to leadership positions whether taking over a single project or a whole "section-load" of them like John. This entire book is devoted to project leadership issues, but here we address three more. The first set of issues we address is the expectations others have of a project leader. Project leaders are called on to play many, often conflicting, roles for various stakeholders. We identify many of the more common role expectations and offer some advice about them.

The second set of issues focuses on leadership needs as they are tied to running a project. Project leaders need to lead differently depending on a project's stage in its life cycle. John, for example, will need to lead his project teams and work with the project's other stakeholders differently because the projects are at different points in their life cycles. We examine the different needs that projects require depending on their life cycle stage and what leaders should do to address those needs.

The final set of issues we address are the leadership needs of individual project members. Project personnel come and go on projects and need different kinds of leadership depending on their "job maturity" in doing the project's work. We finish this chapter by discussing individual project member leadership needs and how best to develop project staff.

The Roles of a Project Leader

Organizational leaders are expected to play a role just like everyone else. The leadership role, however, is complex, and different people have very different, often conflicting expectations of a leader. Because the leadership role is so critical to project success, we examine some of the more typical expectations stakeholders have of a project leader. We conclude by suggesting how leaders might negotiate some of the expectations stakeholders have of them.

The roles organizational leaders play have been studied for some time. Two particularly well-known and appropriate studies are those done by Henry Mintzberg[1] and Luthans and Lockwood.[2] Although Mintzberg focused on higher-level managers and Luthans and Lockwood focused on supervisors, their works have elements in common that are particularly applicable to project managers. They are integrated here with an eye toward the role demands of project leaders. We classify them into those role expectations held by external and internal stakeholders.

External Role Requirements

Figurehead and Spokesperson

By the nature of their position, project leaders are the figureheads of their projects. They are called on to represent their projects at most if not all public functions. It is important, then, for project leaders to display proper demeanor in all public venues. Stakeholder and public judgments of the project and its team are influenced a great deal by the demeanor and behavior of its chief representative.

As the chief representative of the project, leaders are also called on to be their project's spokesperson whether giving formal presentations of the project before large groups or speaking one-on-one with individual stakeholders. It is important for project leaders to be up to date on the status of their projects and be able to communicate the progress, needs, and benefits of their projects to external stakeholders when required.[3]

Liaison and Monitor

In the last chapter, we explored the key position project leaders occupy in the larger network of project stakeholders. Because of that position, most if not all project business is conducted through project leaders in their role as liaison to the project.[4] Project leaders need to actively embrace, develop, and maintain their liaison role not only for the good of their projects but for the good of their own careers as well.

The liaison role has both a formal and informal side to it. Formally, project leaders are called on to do business with suppliers, clients, management, and the public, among other stakeholders. Informally, project leaders are often expected to socialize with stakeholders to develop closer ties with them. Many project leaders are less comfortable performing this role, and socializing can be quite time consuming. Shareholder concerns, problems, and opportunities for the project, however, are often first encountered, and can be dealt with more effectively, in these venues.

The project leader also plays a monitoring role. The project network is a principal source of information about stakeholder needs, concerns, resources, and intentions with regard to the project. The project leader needs to continually monitor this network to get important project information, anticipate project problems, and take advantage of opportunities as they arise.

Champion and Negotiator

Project leaders are often expected to be the champions of the projects they lead. Project leaders must be able to communicate the benefits and needs of their projects in terms that speak to stakeholder interests. Working with their ties in the larger project network, leaders also need to help members of their project team resolve difficulties they may encounter outside the team.

Because of their position, stakeholders turn to project leaders as the chief negotiator for the project. The negotiation role is particularly pronounced in the early stages of a project. When stakeholders first come together, all project parameters—scope, costs, and schedule—are open for negotiation.[5] The project leader's key objective in these negotiations is to ensure project success. What success means and what it requires need to be realistically matched.

Negotiations also occur throughout the execution of the project. Stakeholders often ask for more products or for other project changes as they clarify earlier expressions of their needs. Project leaders may have to adapt to these adjustments, known as scope creep, but work to make sure that they get the additional time and resources to do so.

Controller

Clients and higher management in the host organization expect project leaders to control their projects. Essentially, this means that the project is expected to proceed as planned, producing deliverables according to specifications, in line with the budget, and on schedule. Problems of a tactical nature are generally expected to be handled within the project itself. Strategic problems may arise, however, to threaten the project's deliverables, costs, schedule, or other outcomes. Because projects are unique endeavors, strategic problems are not uncommon—the more unique and complex the project, the more common the problems. This rarely eases client and higher-management concerns, however. Project leaders need to monitor their projects carefully to spot emerging problems early and deal with them. If they need to be brought to the attention of stakeholders, plans should be spelled out about how control of the project can be regained and what will be needed to do so.

Internal Role Requirements

Planner and Resource Allocator

The project leader is expected to take the lead on all project planning. Although others may help in developing project plans, the responsibility for planning lies with the project leader. Team members look to the project leader to make sure project plans are viable. Project planning, moreover, is an ongoing process in project work. As a project unfolds, it becomes apparent that the best laid plans have not been able to anticipate every eventuality. Project leaders are expected to look ahead in the project to spot and plan for unanticipated needs and changes.

Much the same can be said for the allocation of project resources. Initial project plans address allocation issues. As the project moves forward, however, the project leader must often shift resources from one activity to another to keep the project on schedule. Experienced project team members know that resource reallocations are often required. That awareness, however, does not completely ease their disappointment of having to do the same tasks (or more) with less. It is important, then, that the project leader informs his or her team as soon as possible when resources need to be reallocated and to tell those involved why such changes are necessary.[6]

Coordinator

Although coordination is an ongoing need in general management, when activities reach a steady state, coordination needs can be met with standard operating procedures. Despite all the efforts made in project planning, steady states are rare in projects, and coordination requires much more real-time work. Leaders will find that they need to meet often with their project teams and individual project members to keep the project coordinated. Time needs to be set aside, then, for project meetings as part of the project plan itself.[7]

Problem Solver

Because projects are unique endeavors, project leaders are generally confronted with a constant stream of problems. Although project leaders should develop and empower their teams to solve problems as they arise, the ultimate authority and responsibility for problem solving lies with the project leader.

Few people like problems, and it is only natural to try to ignore or hide them. Project leaders, however, need to develop another mindset with the project team: Bring up problems before they get out of hand. With proper development and empowerment of the project team, team members will bring both problems and proposed solutions. Proposed solutions will need the consent of project leaders, however, because they are more aware of the ramifications of both the problem and the proposed solution on other components of the project.

Team Leader

Teams expect their leaders to lead them. They expect their leaders to take the lead in all the major task and operational decisions of the project from planning to closedown. Teams also often expect their leaders to take the lead in handling the social-psychological issues that arise in every project. There are an endless number of social-psychological issues that confront project leaders, but motivation, discipline, and conflict are some of the most common. Making sure to reward good work is the more pleasant part of the motivational role component. Surprisingly, it is often overlooked, and the consequences of doing nothing can have quite a negative effect. Disciplining is one of the more difficult leadership responsibilities. The team expects project leaders to spot and address lower-performing members in a productive way. Here, too, there are important negative effects of doing nothing. There is a high potential for conflict in any project because of the stresses and strains of the project itself. The project's demanding schedule, its unanticipated problems, and the dependencies team members have on one another to accomplish their own work are only a few examples of project stressors. The leadership role calls for the project leader to intervene in these situations as they begin to arise and resolve them so the project moves forward productively.

Project leaders are often so focused on task responsibilities that they can miss social-psychological problems until they grow to the point that they begin to undermine the project's performance. Leaders need to keep lines of communication open not just on task issues but on social-psychological ones as well. Is coordination becoming difficult? Is communication within the team and with the project leader beginning to suffer? Is absenteeism on the rise? Are team members complaining about one another instead of task problems? These kinds of issues often signal people problems. As with task problems, dealing with social-psychological problems early in their development is far easier than dealing with them later.

Clarifying the Leadership Role

It is easy to become overwhelmed with the project leader's responsibilities. Most project leaders will attest, however, that the real problem is the conflicting and widely different expectations that team members and external stakeholders have of them. The project leader's role will never be an easy one to play. Project leaders, however, can take the lead in helping to *make* their own role rather than just *take* the role expectations of others. To do this, project leaders need to discuss their role expectations with critical stakeholders (e.g., clients, managers, and team members). Project leaders, for example, should set aside time during the launch of a project to discuss their expectations of the team and to solicit and discuss the team's expectations as well. The same can be said of working with managers and clients—first probing their expectations, then discussing what can be done to address their most important needs. Although confronting and discussing role expectations will never solve all role problems, it can go a long way to reducing them to manageable levels.

Project Leadership and the Project's Life Cycle

Leadership needs and requirements differ depending on the stage of a project's life cycle. We examine the early stages of initiation and planning first followed by the leadership needs in a project's launch. The execution phase is examined from two perspectives: internal team leadership needs and external stakeholder needs. The project's closing stage needs to address concerns of the client, the host organization, and the project team. These stages become more apparent and distinct the longer the project's time horizon. In shorter projects, they can blur into one another but their leadership needs remain the same.

The Early Stages: Initiation and Planning

The initial stages of initiation and planning begin when a project leader first learns of a client's project. It ends when the leader finishes planning and organizing the project and turns to producing the project's deliverables. Chapters 2, 3, and 4 are dedicated to the issues involved in the early planning stages of a project. We summarize and elaborate on a few of their key points to address three leadership objectives in the early stages of project work. The first is to make sure the project is doable. The second is to organize the project. The third is to begin acquiring the resources necessary to carry out the project.

There are at least two key issues leaders must address to make sure a project is viable. The first is determining the project's objectives and deliverables and their requirements in terms of the project's parameters—its work scope, costs, and schedule. The second is to develop agreement between the client, higher management, and the project leader over these issues so key stakeholders accept and support the project as planned.

Throughout the initial stages in particular, leaders will be called on to address the project's parameters as negotiations about the project go forward. Often the most challenging initial task is to establish the project's deliverables. Clients often have only a vague idea of what they need to address the problems they face. Project leaders are called on, then, to help clients express and clarify their needs in terms of what a project can produce.

As a project's deliverables begin to be defined, the parameters of the project emerge as issues—the work required, the costs, and the timeline. As they do, pressures begin to mount between clients, the host organization, and the project leader as to their specifics and what it is reasonable to expect. Project leaders need to expect such pressures and negotiate the critical requirements that will make a project feasible.

Once project stakeholders have agreed to the project's components, the leader's attention turns to more detailed planning for the project. Attention turns, as well, to organizing the project. Organizing needs to be done from the broader project level to the level of individual work. At the broader project level, the project's basic organizational structure needs to be determined. The major phases of project production are laid out as well as the project's authority structure—what positions will have responsibility and authority for accomplishing the various components of project work.[8] At the more detailed levels of the project, client and other project-relevant deliverables are broken down to specific task deliverables required from individual project members. The work breakdown structure and project scheduling covered in Chapters 3 and 4 are extremely useful tools to use in accomplishing these tasks.

Finally, the leader is called on to set up and align project resources. The key resource in any project is the project team itself. Although some project leaders have a standing staff, many do not. In the latter case, as a project begins to emerge, leaders should start thinking about and recruiting key project personnel. The earlier this can be done the better for at least three reasons. First, there is generally competition for good staff. The earlier leaders can recruit them, the more likely they will be available. Second, key staff can serve as expert advisors in the project's planning. Third, as the project moves forward, key staff involved in planning can better assist in the project's launch and execution.

The project leader needs to think about securing other project resources as well. Those resources that are critical and more difficult to obtain command a leader's greatest attention. In-house resources may fall into this category. Those who have authority over the use of these resources are rarely happy about letting others use them. The earlier problems of resource commitment can be addressed, the better.

Involvement in the early stages of a project provides leaders with two important outcomes. The first is the opportunity to shape the project in ways leaders believe are best for the project. The second is to develop a deep understanding of the project that will serve as the foundation for future project direction and control. The physical manifestation of that deep understanding is the project plan. In some cases, projects are simply handed to leaders to execute, and they have little opportunity to shape them. In those cases, it is imperative for leaders to still develop a deep understanding of the project, its components, and the rationale behind them.

Project Launch

Project launch begins with the actual work on the client's deliverables. In this stage, leaders focus their attention on the project team. The short-term objectives are to orient the team and have it begin work on project deliverables. The longer term goal is for the project team to assume management of the project's work as they move into the execution stage of the project.[9]

When a project is first launched, project members generally look to their leaders to tell them about the project and what they are to do. The more leaders demonstrate knowledge of the project, its needs, and their ability to handle them, the more confidence team members will have in them.

Initially, leaders should summarize the important outcomes of the initiation and planning stages so the team can be brought up to speed. The objective is to help the project team understand the project and their roles in it. The project's mission, objectives, and client deliverables should be presented first. This lays out the basic directions and goals of the project. Next, the project's work and organizational structure are laid out. This tells the team how the goals will be achieved and what role each team member will play. This is an opportune time, as well, to present the basic norms of the project. Producing quality work on schedule is a pivotal project norm to advance. A "no-surprise" norm might be another; when team members see problems ahead, they need to let their leaders know as soon as possible.

Once an overall picture of the project is conveyed, progressive detail is given down to the individual member level—the specific deliverables each member is to provide and when. Greater attention is given to deliverables due early in the project. With small projects and teams, this might be done all at once with everyone present. With larger projects, this might require a series of meetings focusing on different components of the project.

During the initial launch, team members desire, and leaders should adopt, a more "telling" or directive style of leadership. The leader's objectives are to inform the team about the project and their roles in it, and to get project work moving ahead. Team members generally have these same desires and expect their leaders to proceed in this manner. Although questions of clarification will help the team move forward, arguments about the rationale behind the planning and execution of the project are usually better handled one-on-one.[10]

Once the project has been explained to and is understood by the project team, leadership attention needs to focus on initial team and team member work. Leaders should pay attention to both work and resource needs. New task work requires close attention until the team moves up the learning curve. Early production problems, for example, may well require attention so initial work can proceed more productively. This is also a time to address any issues of task commitment. Focus and time on task are two behaviors leaders should look for in the project team. In terms of resource flow, leaders need to make sure resources and other help are available when needed. As the team settles into their work, the project moves into its execution stage.

Project Execution

Project execution begins with the delegation of project tasks to the project team and ends when the project enters its final, closing stage. The objective is to keep the project on track and the project plan is the project leader's principal task tool (with its list of deliverables, work breakdown structure, schedule, budget, and the like). To keep the project on track, leaders are called on to accomplish a number of tasks during the execution phase of a project—the more so the more complex the project. Our focus is on monitoring and controlling project work in the project team and tracking the more critical external stakeholders: the client, higher management, resource suppliers, and regulators. Our discussions also focus more on the behavioral side of project leadership than on the technical issues of project control.

The Project Team

There is an old management saying: "You need to inspect what you expect." Leaders need to monitor project work to make sure it is progressing as needed. Just how leaders monitor their projects and supervise their teams may be more a matter of leadership style than leadership principles.[11] Too-close supervision can get in the way of good performance and staff development. Too little supervision can let the project get so far off track that it is difficult, if not impossible, to complete it on time or on budget.

As a rule, project leaders should not wait too long to see concrete, measurable progress being made on a project task, component, or phase. People have a natural tendency to put off work until nearing the time for its delivery to attend to other pressing matters. Sometimes, too, staff will wrestle with project problems until too much time has passed before seeking help. When project staff must produce a concrete product on the way to larger project deliverables, however, it becomes much more difficult to put things off for too long. If, for example, a project job requires the results of a particular study, the design of the study, the acquisition of study resources, data gathering, analysis, and the writing of the final report are all subtasks that must be done to produce the study. The results of each subtask, then, can become a concrete deliverable that can be reviewed on the way to the ultimate product of the study itself. This kind of work breakdown is best done in the earlier stages of planning and conveyed to the project team as part of the project package in the project's launch.

Project monitoring involves comparing what has been accomplished to what should have been accomplished by a certain time, and the project plan is the leader's principal tool. On many smaller, less complex projects, monitoring project deliverables is enough—comparing what has been produced to what should have been produced according to the schedule.

Cost analysis becomes more important on more complex projects and those done for profit. One way to monitor costs is to simply compare the actual costs of project work completed (i.e., actual cost of work performed) to what was budgeted for the work (i.e., budgeted cost of work performed). When actual costs exceed budgeted costs, there is cause for concern—the more so the larger the difference.

Both costs and progress can be monitored using earned value analysis. The budgeted cost of work actually performed is a cost measure of how far along project work has progressed. At any particular date on the schedule, this figure can be compared to scheduled costs (i.e., the budgeted costs of work scheduled to be done by that date). This comparison will show, in dollar terms, how much *actual* project work is ahead or behind *scheduled* work. Although earned value analysis focuses only on the cost dimension of projects, it is a common method used to monitor complex projects. Cost deviations in actual versus budgeted costs or budgeted costs and scheduled costs serve as triggers for deeper investigations. The particulars of earned value analysis are beyond the scope of this chapter, but they are presented in more detail in Appendix B.

When project progress begins to slip within the team, leaders need to consider at least four potential causes: organizational, work-related, resource, and personnel problems. Organizational problems generally reside in the project's organizational structure. One common problem is that the work breakdown structure failed to lay out the project's true work scope—the work that needed to be done. Another common organizational problem is poor scheduling of project staff.

Work-related problems arise from the work itself. Technical problems, for example, may take longer to solve than anticipated. Another example might be problems working with external stakeholders (e.g., auditees resisting audits or trainees not acquiring skills as quickly as anticipated).[12] Resource problems occur from the interruption or poor scheduling of critical resource flow (e.g., equipment, materials, or information).

Personnel problems are usually problems of ability or commitment. Problems of ability lie in the required knowledge, skills, and abilities to do project work (e.g., lack of experience or adequate training). Problems of commitment are seen in terms of effort and time on task. Sources of commitment problems can lie in competing demands made on staff time, issues of morale, or simply the personal choice of staff members not to participate at needed levels of performance.

When diagnosing the causes of project problems, leaders need to be aware of at least two common sources of error. The first is called egocentric bias.

People generally attribute success to their own efforts and failure or problems to forces outside themselves. Leaders can encounter this bias when working with others to find the causes of project problems. The second source of error is internal attribution bias. Supervisors tend to attribute the source of performance problems internally to workers—to their abilities or their commitment—rather than to external factors beyond the worker's control (e.g., the flow of resources needed to do the work). Quite often, the real source of problems lies outside the immediate control of individual workers.

The focus of concern for the project leader, of course, is getting the project back on schedule. Immediate corrective action involving the shifting of resources might be needed to do so, including personnel shifts as well as other resource reallocations. Once the project is back on track, however, the leader should carefully consider the true causes of the problem or the same kind of problem may arise again and again.

External Stakeholders

Project success depends a great deal on how well project leaders deal with external stakeholders.[13] We focus on four stakeholders who are particularly important to the execution stage of the project: clients, higher management, resource suppliers, and regulators.

Clients generally want to see the project proceed as planned. The extent to which they require communications varies. Some clients require quite frequent updating; others simply wait for the project's deliverables. Most clients want at least some progress reports at critical junctures or milestones of the project.

Sometimes clients will desire additional work to be done as new opportunities emerge. Leaders need to be clear about the additional costs such work will require. Other times, projects encounter problems and clients must be approached for additional resources or time. The risks of these kinds of problems need to be anticipated in the early planning stages of a project and clearly communicated to clients. When problems do emerge, leaders need to give their clients as much advance notice as possible and convey concrete plans to minimize the adverse effects of those problems.

Managers in the host organization also want to see the project proceed as planned. At times, higher management may wish to move resources from a leader's project to use in other projects. Project leaders need to detail how this will affect the project so that management can get a clear idea of the ramifications of its actions. Through all such negotiations with both clients and higher management, the project leader wants to keep on good working terms so that the project moves ahead and is received well.[14]

Projects often depend on getting resources from external suppliers and passing certain requirements by external regulators. Project leaders need to check with suppliers about the resources required before they are actually needed. How much lead time is required depends on how well the supplier has delivered in the past. New suppliers of critical resources need to be carefully tracked. Required regulatory reviews also need close attention and careful preparation because certification is often critical to project progress. Both suppliers and regulators are pulled in many different directions by demands of their own, and any particular project can drop from their attention. Making sure they know of and will fit into the project's schedule is worth the effort.

Project Closing

This phase begins when the project begins winding down to final project delivery and ends with a project review by the project leader working with a few critical stakeholders. The objectives are to close the project to the satisfaction of all critical stakeholders and to learn the important lessons the project has taught the project team.

The final phase of a project is typically hectic as the project staff hurries to complete final contract requirements. During this period, it is easy to forget important details and activities that are not directly and substantively related to the main project deliverables. In terms of the client, a simple checklist is a very nice tool to make sure all the bases are covered in a project's closedown.[15] As the project nears the end of the execution phase, all project leads should produce checklists for their own area of operations. These should be constructed with the full participation of project staff to minimize things that might be forgotten. One area requiring particular attention—simply because it is so often overlooked—is the administrative side of the project. Reports often need to be produced, presentations given, payroll and budgets finalized for the host organization, signatures attained, and the like. High on the list is meeting with clients personally to make sure that they are satisfied with the project's deliverables.

The final act of closing a project is done when the project has effectively closed down. That is a time to do an after-action review. In the military, after-action reviews and reports are a principal means for institutional learning—to make sure the lessons taught by the action stick. Project leaders need to review the project once it has closed down to make sure they, too, have learned the lessons taught by the project.[16] When reviewing who will participate in such a review, care needs to be taken that the exercise remains a developmental one, not an opportunity to vent grievances—old or new. Participants should be chosen who can offer candor, insight, and a wide range of perspectives but who are committed to learning, not advancing other agendas.

After-action reviews can cover a wide range of topics. Broadly considering what was both successful and in need of future change can be a good start. Focusing on specific aspects of the project, including administrative and managerial issues as well as the technical work, can help confront issues normally overlooked. Reviewing who were strong and less strong performers can help leaders in future recruiting. Reviewing where things went well with important stakeholders and where improvements might be made can also help leaders deal with them better in the future as well as attend to any leftover tensions.

Project Leadership and Individual Project Members

One quite common characteristic of project work is that personnel often come and go throughout the project as needed. Some staff, of course, may come with the project's launch and leave only at the project's close. Others, however, are often needed for shorter periods during one project phase or another.

When project personnel first come onboard a project, they embark on a job cycle of their own. Initially, they know relatively little about the project and what will be required of them. At these times, they tend to require a fair amount of leadership attention. Later, as they mature in their jobs, less attention is usually required.

Hersey, Blanchard, and Johnson's Situational Leadership theory offers project leaders some good ideas and practical advice about how to best lead individuals through this job cycle.[17] Their model is a stage model of leadership suggesting that project members mature in their jobs through various stages and that different kinds of leadership are needed at each stage. All new project members go through all stages according to Hersey et al., but some, depending on their prior experience, go through them more quickly.

Hersey et al.[18] suggest that whenever someone new joins a project team, he or she needs to be led with a more directive style of leadership. This style of leadership is aimed at orienting the new person to his or her role and getting performance up to speed as quickly as possible. It is also aimed at establishing the leader's authority—that he or she is in charge. New project members tend to need this kind of direction from a task point of view, but they tend to desire it from a people point of view as well. Most new project members want to know what is required of them and to begin their work as soon as possible.

As people settle into their project jobs and become more productive, leaders are advised to discuss with them the rationale behind their jobs and the larger project picture within which their job fits. This helps them mature more in their jobs by becoming more aware of how the project as a whole is organized and the role their work and the work of others play in it. This knowledge and information empowers them with the knowledge to make more important project-related decisions.

The next shift in leadership Hersey et al.[19] advise is to allow maturing workers to participate more in the project's decisionmaking. As problems arise and choices need to be made, participation gives project personnel on-the-job training in how to make good job-related judgments and decisions.

Finally, Hersey et al.[20] advise the leader to delegate project work entirely to those who demonstrate the ability and willingness to take it on. Although leaders will certainly keep tabs on things, delegation allows project leaders to attend to the many other tasks that confront them.

It is easy to see the parallel between Hersey et al.'s[21] leadership model and the prescriptions given previously regarding project leadership and the project's life cycle. Similar parallels can be seen with the stages of team development covered in Chapter 5. Across all these discussions, leaders are advised that different kinds of behaviors are needed from them to attend to the constantly changing needs of the project, the project team, and its members. This sums up fairly well the challenges and excitement of project leadership.

Summary

Although project leadership entails many demands, we focused on three clusters of them. The first was the roles leaders are expected to play vis-à-vis their position as project leader. The second was the different kinds of leadership needed during the various stages of a project. The third was how best to lead individual project staff as they come and go on a project.

Project leaders are expected to play many roles external to their projects. Two are figurehead and spokesperson. As a figurehead, project leaders are expected to represent the project in all appropriate public functions, and they should be aware that their behavior and demeanor will reflect on their projects. As the project's figurehead, leaders are also expected to be the spokesperson for their projects. How well they present their projects to others will convey how well stakeholders think about their project and how well they think they are being led. Project leaders also play liaison and monitor roles for their projects. Most formal business and informal contacts with the project are conducted through project leaders in their liaison role. Because project leaders are so involved with external stakeholders, they are uniquely positioned to monitor the project's environment to keep abreast of relevant project information. Project leaders are also expected to champion their projects to stakeholders in ways that get their projects the resources and support they need. Because of their positions, project leaders generally play a key negotiating role for their projects. Finally, clients and higher management expect project leaders to play a controller role for their projects. They are expected to keep the project moving forward as planned—staying on budget and on schedule. Leaders should handle the more routine problems of a tactical nature in the context of the project. Larger strategic problems should be brought to the attention of the appropriate stakeholder with plans for their remediation.

Project leaders are also expected to play a variety of roles for their project team. In their planning role, leaders are expected to take the lead on all project planning during the early stages of a project and whenever new plans are needed to adjust for project changes. Project leaders are also the key resource allocators for their projects. Project resources often have to be reallocated during a project, and the leader must take the lead in deciding those reallocations. Project leaders are also expected to coordinate project work and help solve its problems. Coordination is an ongoing challenge in project work because a steady state is rarely achieved for long. Project leaders are also expected to take the lead in problem solving. Problems are an expected component of any project because projects are, by definition, unique endeavors. Technical and operational problems go with the territory, and project leaders need to help and empower their teams to solve them. The solution of technical problems may well lie outside the leader's area of expertise. Even so, all solutions that will affect the larger project need to be authorized by the leader. Finally, project leaders also play a team leader role. This role has both a task and social-psychological component that leaders need to address.

By definition, roles are the expectations that others have of a role holder. Those expectations can vary across those who have them and, in the case of project leaders in particular, are often in conflict. Project leaders also have their preferences for how they would like to fill the expectations that press on them. It is important, then, for leaders to negotiate and clarify the role expectations stakeholders have of them.

Project leadership requirements change depending on the stage in a project's life cycle. Leader involvement in the early initiation and planning stages of a project is important for at least two reasons: to help shape the project and to develop a deep understanding of it for future direction and control. The leader's first responsibility is to clarify the objectives and deliverables of a project. The next obligation is to make sure the project is doable—that the work scope, costs, and time allocations are realistic. These project parameters are best established with leaders in their role as project negotiators. Once a project's parameters are established, leaders turn to organizing their projects. The principal tools for organizing are the work breakdown structure and the project's schedule. Finally, the project leader needs to acquire and align project resources. The most important resource is the project team itself. The earlier leaders can begin assembling the key members of the project team the better. Team members can assist in planning and, as a consequence, participate more fully in the project's launch. Earlier recruitment also increases the probability of getting qualified key personnel.

The project's launch is a particularly critical event in its life cycle. The short-term objective is to make sure project work is properly begun. The longer term objective is to lay the foundation so that project work can be delegated to the project team during the project's execution phase. Leaders need to demonstrate their knowledge and command of the project during this critical period, and project teams expect them to do so. Summarizing the important objectives of the project, how they will be achieved, and who on the team is responsible for what aspects of the project can help achieve these objectives. Once work has begun on project tasks, leaders need to pay attention to both task and resource needs. Task attention focuses on whether project tasks have been initiated properly. Resource attention focuses on making sure resources are flowing as they should.

The primary leadership objective of project execution is to keep the project on track. First, leaders need to monitor the work of the project team. This should be done in a way that is neither too close—hurting good performance—nor too loose—letting the project go off track before taking corrective action. Receiving concrete deliverables before too much time has passed in a project is a good method for keeping the project on track. Breaking down larger deliverables into smaller, interim deliverables is one useful way of accomplishing this. Leaders monitor their projects by comparing what should have been accomplished to what actually has been. The project plan with its work breakdown structure, schedule, and project budget are all used as standards for comparison. Smaller projects might focus simply on deliverables—have they been produced on schedule and according to expectations. Larger projects usually monitor costs as well by comparing, for example, budgeted costs to actual costs of project work. Earned value analysis includes the time dimension by adding scheduled costs as a standard for assessment.

Leaders can look to four principal sources of internal project problems: organizational, work related, resource, and personnel. An example of an organizational problem is that the work breakdown structure did not include required work. Work-related problems emerge from the work itself, such as having to overcome technical difficulties. Resource problems are generally tied to the lack of resources when they are needed. Personnel problems are principally problems of ability or commitment. Either the staff does not have the ability to perform the task given to them, or they lack the commitment to do so. Although the leader needs to get the project back on track as soon as possible, searching for the real cause of project problems will help keep them from emerging in the future.

Project leaders also need to track external stakeholders during the execution phase—success depends a great deal on them. Clients want to see the project proceed as planned and sometimes want additional work to be done. Higher management also wants to see the project proceed as planned and sometimes wishes to reallocate resources to other projects. When strategic problems emerge to threaten the project, leaders need to inform their clients and higher management of the problems and provide plans to resolve them. When clients or management desire additional work or the reallocation of resources, leaders need to make very clear how these decisions will affect the project. Because projects depend on outside suppliers and regulators, leaders need to make sure these stakeholders are well integrated into project plans as required.

When projects close, leaders need to make sure that all the products, services, and other outcomes of a project are delivered to the client. Checklists are good tools to use in this regard. Checklists are also good to make sure all requirements have been met with the host organization to close down the project. Finally, leaders should conduct after-action reviews to look back over the project to learn how to perform better in the future.

The leadership needs of project personnel change as they go through their job cycle on a project just as the leadership needs for the project as a whole change as it goes through its life cycle. At first, personnel need and generally desire a more directive style of leadership to orient them to their job and to get them up to speed on project work. As they demonstrate their abilities to handle their jobs, the leader should spend more time letting them know how their work fits into the overall project and how the project as a whole is organized and led. This empowers the project member with the knowledge and information needed to begin making his or her own more important job-related decisions. Leadership should then shift to a more participatory style to further advance the member's job maturity in terms of being able to develop good project judgments and make good decisions about broader project issues. Finally, for those who show the ability and willingness to accept the responsibility, the leader should shift to a more delegative style of leadership, turning his or her attention to other project tasks.

Review Questions

1. Define and identify the expectations of the following roles of a project leader:
   a. Liaison and monitor
   b. Champion
   c. Controller
   d. Planner and resource allocator
   e. Team leader

2. Why should a project leader clarify his or her leadership role?
   a. How should he or she go about doing so?

3. Discuss the various leadership requirements in the following stages of the project's life cycle:
   a. Initiation and planning
   b. Project launch
   c. Project execution
   d. Project closing

Exercises

1. Review the various roles project leaders are called on to play.
   a. Assess your strengths and weaknesses for each of them.
   b. For those roles in which you are not strong, how would you address them in any given project?

2. Identify a project of your own choosing.
   a. Lay out a plan for its initiation and planning.

3. Recall a school or work project that you have recently completed.
   a. Conduct an after-action review of the project.
   b. How would you do things differently if you were the project leader (again)? In addressing this question, review and comment on what occurred in the project as it moved through its various project stages.

Endnotes

1. Mintzberg, H. (1973). *The nature of managerial work.* New York: Harper Row.
2. Luthans, F., & Lockwood, D. L. (1984). Toward an observation system for measuring leader behavior in natural settings. In J. G. Hunt, D. Hosking,

C. A. Schriesheim, & R. Stewart (Eds.), *Leaders and managers: International perspectives on managerial behavior and leadership* (pp. 117–141). New York: Pergamon Press.

3. It is also important for external stakeholders to get a consistent message about the project. For this reason, external communications are often restricted to the project leader. If other project members are required to interact with external stakeholders, it is important that the project leader be present if possible or thoroughly debriefed if not.

4. Often, team members will work with external stakeholders as well. It is important in these interactions that the project leader is kept thoroughly informed of important project business.

5. An excellent source for negotiation is: Fisher, R., Ury, W., & Patton, B. (1991). *Getting to yes: Negotiating agreement without giving in.* New York: Penguin Books.

6. Social accounts or the explanations leaders give followers for decisions that involve loss have been well researched in the organizational justice literature. Laying out the causes that required the change and the project goals that will be addressed by the change can help dampen the disappointment and anger team members may have about the change. It may be that such accounts cannot be given immediately, but leaders should remember to give them as soon as possible.

7. Meetings, of course, are legitimate project activities to the extent they add value to the project over and above the opportunity costs of those who must attend them. Project leaders are expected to weigh those costs and benefits carefully.

8. There is an old management dictum that when more than one person has responsibility for a task, no one has responsibility for it. Although project work often requires the efforts of many, one person needs to be accountable for getting the task done.

9. The working assumption here is that a project's launch occurs with the entire team all at once. In many projects, team members join the project in different phases. The project needs to be launched to newcomers as they arrive—providing them the information they need and making sure initial work is proceeding as planned.

10. Quite often, concerns of project members are not raised in this early stage of project work. As the team moves into its storming stage, however, more concerns and disagreements about the rationale behind project issues may arise (see Chapter 5). Project leaders should not necessarily take this as insubordination but as legitimate participation over valid concerns that need to be addressed. This is often best done one-on-one.

11. Fiedler, F. E. (1967). *A theory of leadership effectiveness.* New York: McGraw-Hill.

12. These kinds of problems need to be anticipated as sources of project risk early in planning and clearly communicated to clients and higher management.

13. Ancona, D. G., & Caldwell, D. (1992). Bridging the boundary: External activity and performance in organizational teams. *Administrative Science Quarterly, 37,* 634–665.

14. An excellent source for client and higher-management negotiations is Fisher et al. (1991).

15. Building contractors often use a punch list to finish off their projects. They get together with their clients to review the property and, together, negotiate a list of final things that need to be done to finish the job. The company of a project manager I know does something similar. Managers do a computer word search for all elements of their contracts that have the phrases "The company will," or "The company shall. . . . " These phrases were placed in the contract specifying deliverables, and the word search constructs a check-off list for them.

16. As mentioned previously, lessons are really learned throughout the project and should be used as they are acquired. After-action reviews, however, offer the opportunity to wrap them up given the full advantages of hindsight.

17. Hersey, P., Blanchard, K. H., & Johnson, D. E. (1996). *Management of organization behavior: Utilizing human resources* (7th ed.). Englewood Cliffs, NJ: Prentice-Hall. Their ideas are abstracted here and adjusted for project leadership needs.

18. (1996).

19. (1996).

20. (1996).

21. (1996).

8

Writing Project Reports

Introduction	142
The China Report	142
Chapter Overview	142
Know Your Readers and What They Want	143
What Any Reader Wants	144
What Decision Makers Want	144
What Expert Advisors Want	146
What Users and Implementers Want	146
The Project Report	147
The Front End	148
The Cover Page	148
The Letter of Transmittal	148
The Table of Contents	149
Lists of Tables and Illustrations	149
The Executive Summary	149
The Body	150
The Introduction	150
Major Sections and Subsections of the Report	151
Conclusions and Recommendations	152
References and Bibliography	153
The Back End: Supporting Appendices	153
Summary	155
Review Questions	156

Exercises	157
Endnotes	157
Table 8.1: Project Report Check-Off List	154

Introduction

The China Report

Tim Conway and Jennifer Lau had just finished a very tough project for their company, Tech Machine Tools. Tech Machine manufactures high-end precision tool and dye machines used by other companies to produce a wide variety of precision products. Based in Wisconsin, Tech Machines wanted to explore the feasibility of two business ventures. The first was to develop and run another manufacturing facility in southern China. The "economics" seemed attractive to Tech Machine's executives, but they needed an in-depth study of the idea. The second venture was to explore what it would take to break into the market for high-end machine tools in southern China. China's economy was growing at a very promising rate, and Tech Machines would like to "get in on the action" as Dave Reynolds, the CEO, put it. The idea was to gain a foothold somewhere in that region and use it to expand to other areas of China.

Tim and Jennifer were having a cup of coffee together by way of celebration for completing the project when their conversation turned to their last project task—producing a project report. As they discussed this last task, it began to dawn on them how important yet difficult the task was. It was important because information in the report itself would be used as the basis for Tech Machine executives' deciding whether to invest millions of dollars and perhaps years of effort into a major strategic move—one that would greatly help or hurt the company. The report would be important, too, if the decision was made to move ahead. Those who would be charged with carrying out the venture would look to the report for guidance and the information they would need to make the right decisions. If these issues were not daunting enough, Tim and Jennifer realized that each one of them thought that the other had the knowledge and experience they would need to write up the final report—neither did.

Chapter Overview

Project reports can differ a great deal from one another in a number of ways. They differ in their purpose, their formats, and their formality to name just a few. In this chapter, we will focus on the kind of project report facing Tim and Jennifer. They will need to produce a formal report with all the "bells and whistles." The purpose of the project report, furthermore, is not to simply present what the project found. The report is an important project deliverable itself that is designed to be used. First, it is to provide the information necessary to help decision makers decide whether to invest a great deal of time, money, and resources into opening up operations in a foreign country. Second, if that decision is made, the report will likely be used as an initial source of information to help those who will actually embark on that venture.

There is a wide variety of people who might read a project report, but most of the time they fall into three basic categories: decision makers, their advisors, and those who might use the report to help implement its recommendations. We begin this chapter by focusing on what each type of reader wants from a project report.

Formal reports like the one facing Tim and Jennifer can seem daunting at first. Formal reports, however, have at least one saving grace: They all have more or less the same structure. They have a "front end" with various kinds of material, a main body, and a "back end" with supporting appendices. The rest of this chapter will be devoted to working our way through these components, discussing what belongs in each of them.

Know Your Readers and What They Want

Writing specialists, authors, and readers alike make one recommendation to report writers above all others: Know your reader—know what they want and how they want it delivered. Endless reports have been tossed aside because this simple recommendation was not followed. Although the advice is sound, its implementation is often difficult. When we write project reports, we tend to address our own views of the project and what we consider most important.

Generally speaking, the readers of a project report are some of the same stakeholders who have had an interest in the project all along. The time to get to know your readers, then, is not at the end of the project but from its very beginning. Project leaders need to communicate with their stakeholders all the way through a project. In their conversations, interim reports, and presentations, project leaders need to consider what stakeholders consider most important and how they want information presented to them.

We have discussed stakeholders before in terms of the roles they play: client, host manager, team members, and the like. Report readers also step into roles, and the roles they play largely determine what they are looking for in a project report and how they want it delivered. One of the most important roles is the decision maker. Decision makers will look to your report to help them make the decisions they are faced with in the future. A related role is the advisor. Advisors are often experts who help decision makers assess the quality of a report, its information, and its findings and outcomes. Still a third role is played by users or implementers of the report. Implementers look to the report to help them with the tasks they face when moving forward with report recommendations. Of course, the same reader may play all these roles, but we will examine what each wants from a report separately. We begin, however, by discussing what any reader wants from a report.[1]

What Any Reader Wants

Most readers of a project report have some general things they would like writers to keep in mind.

- *Readers want things simple.* They do not have the time or inclination to work at understanding what you are trying to say. Keep sentences simple and vocabulary straightforward; avoid jargon and acronyms that are not familiar to your readers. Keeping things simple, however, does not mean ignoring important elements and details needed by the reader.

- *Readers want what they want.* They want to skip to things that are of interest and importance to them. You need to make sure you cover what is important to your key readership and help them find it in your report.

- *Readers want what they want quickly.* They want to be able to skip and skim the material as they see fit. Reports are best written to facilitate quick reading in such a way that key ideas and components are gotten across to all readers with more detail quickly available to those who want it. Layout, table of contents, graphics, and the use of bullets and headings go a long way toward achieving these ends.

- *You want your readers to have confidence in your abilities.* Developing your relationship with key stakeholders during the course of the project is the best way to build stakeholder trust. How well the report is written, however, is a key element in maintaining that confidence. Even the best project can be undermined with a poor report. Even difficult projects can come off well with excellent presentations.

What Decision Makers Want

One of your most important readers is the decision maker. Decision makers are those who have the authority to allocate resources to the project and to follow up on any recommendations the report will make. Like any other category of reader, decision makers come in all shapes and sizes. There are at least two common characteristics among them, however, that the writer should keep in mind. First, decision makers are busy people. Although your project may be first and foremost in your mind, it is likely only one of many and varied projects and tasks confronting the decision maker. Second, decision makers are paid to make things happen. As a result, they must translate the information provided to them into concrete courses of action. Authors succeed with decision makers to the extent they help them do this. As a direct result of these two basic characteristics, formal project reports should attend to a number of issues.

• *Give background information quickly.* Because the decision maker is confronted with many tasks and projects, you will want to remind him or her quickly about your project. The background information needed generally includes the problem the project is addressing and the basic objectives of the project. Presenting the project's mission statement and project objectives will usually be enough. The basic activities of the project might also be included in your review of background information if you think it is required. This information is usually given in the first paragraph of an executive summary and the introduction of a formal report.

• *Think and write strategically.* When developing formal reports for decision makers, focus on key strategic issues and information relevant to them. Identify the important decisions facing decision makers and what information they need to make them.

• *Layer information according to detail.* Generally speaking, decision makers do not like to be hit with a lot of detail all at once. They like summaries first and progressively more detail as they need it while moving ahead in their decisionmaking process. This works out well in formal reports because different parts of the report are made for different levels of detail. The executive summary has the least amount of detail. The body of the report has more detail but still basically summarizes and explains the findings of a project. The appendices provide the most amount of detail. Separating out what is detail from what is absolutely necessary is often a difficult task for technical experts in an area. Project leaders need to keep in close contact with their readers, then, to make sure the report provides the level of detail desired.[2]

• *Avoid technical jargon.* Common phrases and vocabulary for a technical expert can be so much incomprehensible jargon to those outside the technical or specialist area. Write using the language and phrasing common to the reader, not to you.

- *Write for their level of expertise.* The expertise of decision makers is often different from that of the project writer. Project reports need to be written to (not down to) the level of expertise of the decision maker.

What Expert Advisors Want

Decision makers often make use of expert advisors to confirm the quality of a project report's content. Whoever plays the role of expert advisor will likely have expectations of his or her own.

Expert advisors want to have available to them the technical detail behind the report. They expect thorough explanations that are to the point. They may also like to have available the data used in developing the project's product. Quite often, they will examine the references used in the report to make sure the project personnel are up to date and knowledgeable in the areas covered by the project.

Most of the needs expert advisors have for detail are satisfied with the use of supportive appendices. Technical issues covered and summarized in the body of the report should refer to supporting detail in an appropriate appendix. As with all readers, expert advisors want ease of access to supportive detail and ease of review of the data. As the expert advisor reads through the body of the report, provide him or her with the title and page number of the supportive appendix so he or she can easily flip to the material as desired.[3]

What Users and Implementers Want

Many projects are done as a first step for follow-on work. Tim and Jennifer's feasibility study is just one example. If Tech Machine executives decide to go ahead with the venture, those who will lead the effort will turn to Tim and Jennifer's report for help. The project report developed for Linda Swain's Compliance Project in Chapter 3 would likely be used in the future as well. She developed standard operating procedures for state inspections, and those procedures would likely be contained in the appendices of the final report. John's project to open the Baltimore store for Acme Auto in Chapter 2 may also be used by others even if there was no project objective to do so. If the project were deemed a success, a requested follow-on final report might be reviewed in terms of a best practices model for store openings.

Clearly, to the extent that follow-on users may need information from the report, the project leader needs to think of them as important project stakeholders. Sometimes their needs may be modest. In John's Baltimore Project write-up, a few tables and a flow chart of opening tasks may be enough. Sometimes their needs can be met with a little more work. In Linda's case, standalone manuals to prepare for state inspections might be needed. In Tim and Jennifer's case, however, implementers would require a great deal of information. The extent to which the project would be dedicated to addressing those needs should be assessed by project leaders at the beginning of a project and included in all project planning.

The Project Report

Formal project reports tend to have a common structure. That structure is helpful to both writer—who wants to know what to cover—and the reader— who knows what to expect. We cover that structure in three basic parts: the front end, the body of the report, and the back end. The front end of a report covers all material up to the actual body of the report (e.g., the cover page, table of contents, and executive summary). Usually developed at the end of the actual writing of the report, the elements of the front end are, nevertheless, extremely important to the report's success. The body of the report covers the actual discussion of the project itself. It includes an introduction, major sections and subsections of the report's content, the report's conclusions and recommendations, and the reference section or bibliography. The back end of the report includes all the support material for the report in appropriate appendices.

It is important to remember that project reports are technical documents. There is little glamour and creativity to them. Clear and concise writing is the all-too-elusive goal. Almost never are they narratives—they do not tell stories; they simply report findings of the project.[4] Project reports are not marketing documents, either. Even project proposals should reject marketing ploys and gimmicks. Project teams should let the quality of the project report speak for itself. If the proposal or report addresses the needs of the stakeholder in a clear, appropriate, and competent way, the project will sell itself.

All this is not to say that authors should ignore the packaging and presentation of the report. In addition to the technical requirements of report writing (clear concise statements, appropriate use of headings and bullets, appropriate macrostructure of content, and the like), the look of a report also matters. Graphics and illustrations should be pleasing to the eye. Support appendices are often bound separately from the front end and body of the report. This allows the report itself to be read and transported more easily and makes the smaller main report itself look more accessible to a reader than a 6- or 8-inch thick report that includes appendices with it. Such elements do count for making the report more readable, but in the end, a project report is meant simply to present and explain facts and outcomes of the project.

The Front End

The front end of a project report includes its cover page, possibly a letter of transmittal, a table of contents, lists of tables and illustrations, and the executive summary. Each of these begins on a new page.

The Cover Page

The cover page of a project report is straightforward. It begins with the title of the report, gives the authors' names and titles (sometimes this is an organization rather than a person or team), provides the date of transmittal, and includes the name of the people or organization receiving the report.[5]

The title of the project is often the title of the report. Tim and Jennifer's report, for example, might be entitled "Final Report on the Feasibility of Establishing Manufacturing and Marketing Operations in China." At least two common mistakes occur in providing titles. First, some writers want to capture all the elements of a project in its title, which results in a title several lines long (e.g., "Final Report on the Feasibility of Developing Manufacturing Operations in China Inclusive of Supply Chain Considerations, Cost Parameters, and Cultural Aspects as well as Marketing. . . . " Well, you get the idea.). Although exactitude is achieved, the reader knows from the very start that reading the report will be a daunting task. Other writers will often give a report a catchy title in hopes of grabbing the attention of the reader or simply expressing their own creativity. "On Gaining a Foothold in the Mysterious Orient" or a similar title may or may not pique the interest of some readers, but it tells very little about what is inside the report.

The Letter of Transmittal

The letter of transmittal conveys the project report to a specific reader, group, or audience and should follow the normal layout and conventions of a business letter or memo. Opening remarks usually identify the project to the reader. Letters for final reports usually state that the terms of the contract have been met and present one or two key findings or outcomes that are of key interest to the recipient of the letter. It is a good idea to formally acknowledge the help of key stakeholders of the project—particularly those who funded it. Offers of future help might be included (to encourage future business) and contact information provided in case the reader has questions or would like your team to work with them in the future. The letter of transmittal may or may not be bound with the report itself.

The Table of Contents

The table of contents lists the major sections and subsections of the report along with the page numbers where they can be found.[6] The table of contents begins on a separate page with the title of the report at the top followed by the title "Table of Contents."

Beyond the technical requirements of the table of contents (e.g., getting the headings and page numbers right), a table of contents plays a very important role in any project report. Consider for a moment where you first look to see what is inside a book or larger report. It is almost always the table of contents. Because the table of contents is where the reader will look first, it provides the writer with an opportunity let the reader know what is in the report that will be of interest to him or her. It also provides the reader with a quick overview of the report and a map to its contents. With these ideas in mind, the headings used in the report and given in the table of contents should be clear descriptive labels as to the content covered underneath the heading. As with the title of the report itself, overly long technical headings and vague catchy ones are to be avoided.

Lists of Tables and Illustrations

Project reports also list the tables and illustrations in the report. These are listed separately from one another, have their own title (e.g., "List of Tables"), and provide the page numbers where the tables and illustrations can be found.[7]

The Executive Summary

The executive summary is one of the most important components of any project report. A great deal of attention should be given to it. The label "executive summary" conveys the essence of what is being written and for whom. The summary is designed principally for decision makers. Generally these include those who have funded the project and those who will decide what, if any, actions are to be taken based on it. Writers should keep their needs in mind when producing the executive summary (see "What Decision Makers Want" covered previously). Quite often, decision makers read little else besides the executive summary and the report's conclusions and recommendations.

The term *summary* in an executive summary refers to a summary of the project's outcomes or findings. Rarely does this include how the project was done unless the conduct of the project was an integral part of the project itself (e.g., using a particular required approach to a study). Even in these cases, the conduct of the project would be summarized only briefly (e.g., "Using prescribed methods. . . .").

Recal what decision makers generally want to read. The executive summary begins with a very brief introduction of background information: the purpose and objectives of the project along with other information required to help focus the decision maker on what the project was all about. This should take about a short paragraph. The remainder of the summary should summarize the important findings and outcomes of the project. It should conclude with a few of the project's key conclusions and recommendations if any. In general, the executive summary is best kept to a single page, although an executive summary of less than a page that adequately addresses the project is even better. More involved projects may require more than a page.

Because executive summaries are summaries of outcomes for decision makers, they generally do not cover descriptions of the process that was done to develop the outcome or relate stories of who did what. Being terse, summaries do not say explicitly that any of their content is important—it is assumed that if it is in the summary, it must be important. Finally, executive summaries are not venues for advertising how well the project was done or how important its outcomes are to the reader. Given the proper presentation of the facts and outcomes, the reader will see that the project not only was done well but achieved its aims without any sales pitch.

The Body

The body of the project report begins on a new page with the title of the report at the top. It begins with the report's introduction, moves through the major sections and subsections of the report, wraps up with the report's conclusions and recommendations, and ends with the reference section or bibliography.

The Introduction

The introduction of the report provides at least two key background elements of the project. The first is the purpose and objectives of the project and any key information related to them (e.g., for whom the project was done, key constraints). The introductory statement given in the executive summary can be duplicated and elaborated a little more here. A good, serviceable start for an introduction is a purpose statement that mirrors the project's mission statement: "The purpose of this project was to. . . ."

The second element of an introduction is a statement of the project's scope. This would include the project's main objectives and its specific deliverables. A general overview of the project scope is enough for the body of the report with any more required detail given in a supporting appendix. Although most readers generally skim or skip this material, it is a formal statement of what was required and delivered for the project.

Major Sections and Subsections of the Report

The major sections and subsections of the report follow and, together, form the "macro-structure" of the report. Quite often, the project's main objectives and deliverables can help the writer develop the report's macro-structure. The major objectives of the project might be used to structure the major sections of the report, and subsections might deal with second-level objectives or deliverables. In this case, the scope statement given in the introduction can serve as an overview of the report's content. The key here is to "chunk" information in ways that make sense. The structure of the project itself can help writers do just that.

In Tim and Jennifer's report, for example, the body of the report might be broken down into two major sections: "Developing Manufacturing Operations" and "Developing Marketing Operations." Looking into the feasibility of these two ventures were the basic objectives of their project. Subobjectives and deliverables in each of those areas, then, would likely form subsections of the report. For example, when looking into manufacturing operations, Tim and Jennifer may have been charged to consider (a) possible locations, (b) the skilled and unskilled labor market, (c) issues related to the acquisition of plant and materials, and (d) the costs of such an endeavor. Subsections devoted to each of these, then, would be appropriate.

The structure and layout of each section and subsection should promote skimming. Descriptive headings in bold font help the reader quickly identify the location and contents of the sections and subsections of interest to him or her. In each section, information is best chunked into coherent units. For example, each subsection should deal only with related issues, each paragraph with one basic idea. Bullets with descriptive labels (also in bold font) can help the reader identify content of interest quickly.

The body of the report should go into enough detail to cover the issues adequately but leave extensive details and large listings of data to supportive appendices. Admittedly, this can be a tricky call and knowing what the most important readers want will help the writer. In general, though, the body of the report seeks to explain project outcomes—not review lots of data and detail. Concise summaries of information and data in tables and graphs are handy ways of presenting supporting facts and figures. Supportive appendices with more detailed data are identified in the body of the report when the issues are covered. References to appendices should use the name of the appendix and give the page number where the appendix can be found.[8]

Conclusions and Recommendations

Conclusions and recommendations wrap up the report and are one of its most important sections. After reading the executive summary and, perhaps, giving the body of the report a quick scan, many decision makers turn to this section for extended reading and consideration.

Although the conclusions and recommendations of a project are reserved for a relatively small section of the report, they represent some of the most important products the team can provide. The project team has been deeply involved in all aspects of a project of great interest to the client. Only the project team has had full access to all the issues, information, problems, and solutions in the project. The project team, then, is in the best position to analyze the project's results, come to conclusions about them, and to make recommendations to further the client's aims. This section, then, represents one of the most important value-added components of a project, and it requires careful and extended thought.

Conclusions summarize the findings and outcomes of the project, not the content of the report itself—a common mistake. Now that the project is done, what did you find out or discover? What can you conclude about the project's objectives? This section calls on the project leader and team to analyze the project and its objectives and outcomes. Now that they have the experience of the project behind them, what can the project team conclude that is of value to the client, decision maker, or other reader? Tim and Jennifer, for example, might offer conclusions about the initial problems the company might face in setting up manufacturing operations. Conclusions about initial costs, revenue projections, payback period, and critical issues that need to be addressed if the venture is to be successful might also be covered.

Recommendations are courses of action that the project team suggests decision makers should take. Recall that decision makers are paid to make things happen. Your recommendations, then, should be clear, concrete, and action oriented. Tim and Jennifer, for example, might recommend a specific location to set up manufacturing operations and specific vendors to fill the company's needs for equipment and material. They might go on to recommend a number of businesses to approach first as potential buyers of Tech Machine products and recommend different distribution channels. These kinds of recommendations are both concrete and action oriented. Like project objectives, when recommendations are specific, concrete, and actionable, they become useful to decision makers.

References and Bibliography

Most projects use some sources of support for their work. Books, journals, articles, and government documents are a few examples. People contacted and Web sites are others. The reference section is where these materials are listed.[9]

Most decision makers are not too concerned with the reference section. Expert advisors, on the other hand, may well review this section very carefully. They want to make sure you have considered and used all the important and up-to-date studies in the project's area of work. Those who will use or implement some or all of the report's recommendations can find the reference section useful as well. The sources cited may be useful for follow-on work. Keeping these readers in mind, writers may include sources they have come across—but did not incorporate into the report itself—because implementers might find them useful (e.g., how-to manuals, instruments, government documents, and important contacts). Writers can help users as well by providing short annotations of their sources: one- to three-sentence descriptions relevant to user interests. These small efforts can provide real value added at little to no cost to the project team.

The Back End: Supporting Appendices

Appendices supply detailed support material for the final report. They include as well material that might have been mandated by the project but is inappropriate or too detailed for inclusion into the body of the report. The project may have required, for example, that certain studies be conducted. The details of those studies might well be included as appendices so expert advisors can review their quality. Often, projects require the development of material in anticipation of follow-on work (e.g., work procedures or technical manuals). That material is part of the product of the project, and its delivery is often included in the appendices of a report. Finally, the project team may come across useful material as a by-product of its project work (e.g., checklists, questionnaires, operating procedures, schematics, or instruction manuals). These would provide value added to the project's results and be included in the report's appendices.

Table 8.1 includes a list of questions project report writers might find useful. It can serve as a check-off list for some of the major components of more formal end-of-project reports. Although not exhaustive of all considerations, it can serve as an initial point of departure.

Table 8.1   Project Report Check-Off List

There are any number of reports that need to be made for a project. Listed here are a few key questions leaders might ask themselves as they move through the process of writing a more formal end-of-project report. The questions are meant to encourage project leaders to think through the issues involved and to be used as a point of departure rather than as a comprehensive listing.

- Is the title of the report descriptive of its contents?

- Does the table of contents give a good overview of the report? Are the section headings descriptive of their contents? Does the table help the reader to skim the section headings? Can the reader find quickly material that is of interest to him or her?

- Does the executive summary open with a one- or two-sentence description of the project? Does the rest of the summary provide a quick overview of the project's major findings, conclusions, and recommendations? Give serious consideration to excluding all other material from the executive summary.

- Does the introduction of the report provide a quick description of the project? Is a scope statement included listing the major deliverables of the project?

- Is the body of the report arranged in a logical order? Are the section headings descriptive of their contents? Does the report help the reader skim the report so he or she can quickly understand the main issues in the report and focus on those of interest to him or her? Consider the use of bulleted lists where helpful. Consider the use of graphs to display data. Does the report use jargon that intended readers will not understand? Is there too much detail given anywhere in the body? If so, consider moving it to a supporting appendix and providing an overview summary in the body of the report.

- Do the conclusions focus on what has been learned from the project—what can be concluded from it? Are the conclusions clear and logical? Do the conclusions address all issues the client wanted? Resist using the conclusion section to summarize the report itself. If you want a report summary, consider using a separate section for it (e.g., "Report Summary").

- Do the recommendations address all issues the client wanted? Are they action oriented—do they help decision makers make action decisions?

- Does the bibliography or reference section contain references to key material required for the project? Would an expert advisor see those sources needed for the project listed? If the report is to be used as an aid in implementation activities, are sources useful for implementation included?

- Do the technical appendices include everything that was contracted as a deliverable? Are supportive data and information included? Consider including low-cost information that would be helpful to your client.

Summary

Project reports come in all shapes and sizes. Our focus has been on the larger formal report that is given to a client at the project's end. Many of the elements found in those reports are also found in others.

The most important thing authors need to remember about writing project reports is to keep the needs of their readers in mind. The average reader wants the report to state things simply and clearly and to have ready and quick access to information he or she sees as important. Project leaders want readers to have confidence in their abilities as well. How the project is presented in its final report can go a long way toward that end. Decision makers want project reports to help them make decisions about the action objectives that are facing them. They want a quick review of the project's background and information that speaks to the strategic issues facing them. It is best to layer project information so decision makers can access more and more detail as they desire. It is best to avoid technical jargon when writing for decision makers and make sure to write to their level of expertise. Decision makers often look to expert advisors to assess the quality of the project's information. Advisors will want to know that the project team has covered the important sources for the project and will want access to detailed information about it. That level of detail is usually provided in the project report's appendices. Projects are also read by those who are charged with implementing their recommendations. Project leaders should consider such implementers as project stakeholders and produce material useful for them and their activities. Often, this material is placed in the report's appendices as well. To the extent a project is to serve as a first step among many, implementers become a more important stakeholder, and the project needs to include their needs in initial project planning and cost calculations.

Formal project-end reports have a similar structure: a front end, a main body, and a back end. The front end consists of the cover page, the letter of transmittal, the table of contents, lists of tables and illustrations, and the executive summary. The cover page includes the title, the name of who is submitting it, and the submission date. The title should be brief but simple and descriptive of the report's content. The letter of transmittal formally transmits the report to the client and is written much like a business letter or memo. The table of contents is more than a mere listing of section headings. It is the place readers turn first when looking over a report to assess its content quickly. Writers should make sure that the section headings used in the body of the report and listed in the table of contents are simple and descriptive of the issues covered. Lists of tables and illustrations indicate where in the report those tables and illustration are located. The executive summary is one of the most important components of a final report. It summarizes the most important outcomes of the project, and decision makers often depend on it alone for most of their information.

The body of the report includes the introduction, the main sections and subsections of the report, its conclusions and recommendations, and the reference section or bibliography. The introduction should open with the purpose of the project and a statement of its scope: its principal objectives and deliverables. The main sections of the report will often parallel the major and minor objectives of the project itself, reporting findings and outcomes relevant to them. It is important to chunk information in each section so that subsections address connected issues. The general purpose of the main body of a report is not to present the project's detail, but to review its findings and explain them to the reader. Although facts and figures are given in the main body, detailed information is best left to supporting appendices. Conclusions and recommendations form a small part of the report but present some of its most important information—what the project team concludes about the project and its objectives given their deep involvement with it and their recommendations about what should be done now. Conclusions are conclusions about project outcomes—not summaries of the report itself. Recommendations should be specific, concrete, and action oriented.

Although decision makers often do not pay attention to the reference section, expert advisors and implementers do. Advisors want to see if the project team has covered and used the material they should have. Implementers would like sources cited that will help them implement the report's recommendations.

The back end of a project report contains all of its supportive appendices. These include specific products mandated as project deliverables, details of project activities that may need to be reviewed for quality assurance, and any material that the project team may have come across in the course of its work that might be useful for the client. Often, the appendices are bound separately from the main report itself. Some specific appendices may even be bound separately themselves to help readers use them (e.g., manuals produced for later use by implementers).

Review Questions

1. Different readers want different things from a project report.
   a. What does any reader want?
   b. Compare and contrast what decision makers and expert advisors want in a project report.
   c. What do users or those who will implement a report want to see in it?

2. Discuss the importance of the executive summary and what it should and should not contain.

3. Other than indicate where content is located, what function does the table of contents play for the reader?
   a. What considerations should be given to the section titles contained in a table of contents?

4. What are some of the considerations in developing the major sections of the project report's body?

5. What issues are covered in the project report's conclusions and recommendations?

6. What material is typically contained in a project report's supporting appendices?

Exercises

1. Locate a recent student paper you or some friend has written or a paper produced by one of your professors.
   a. Write an executive summary of the paper.
   b. Produce a table of contents for the paper following the guidelines in this chapter. You may have to develop titles for the various sections of the paper. Does the table of contents reveal the substantive content of the paper?

2. Identify any project in which you played a role. This can be a project done for a class or work assignment, a project for a school organization, or one that you developed on your own.
   a. Write an executive summary of the project. Review the summary to see if it reveals what a decision maker would want to know.
   b. If you were to write a report of the project, what sections would be in the body of the report? Label those sections so that they would reveal what the project was about when placed in a table of contents.
   c. Consider what you can conclude from your project and write up a small conclusions section.
   d. If someone else were to repeat your project, what would be your recommendations? Write them up in a small section.

Endnotes

1. Although roles such as these are common ones, William Pfeiffer does a good job of reviewing them. His detailed handling of all kinds of reports makes his work

an excellent reference as well. See Pfeiffer, W. (2003). *Technical writing: A practical approach* (5th ed.). Upper Saddle River, NJ: Prentice Hall. Another excellent book, by William Zinnser, shows quite clearly that even technical reports can be written in an engaging way. See Zinnser, W. (1998). *On writing well: The classic guide to writing nonfiction.* New York: Harper Collins.

2. I recall one presentation put together by some exceptionally talented experts in the field of project risk analysis. The presentation was delivered to some key NATO decision makers about a particular technique for assessing project risk. The presentation had some 47 PowerPoint® slides, beginning with some basic concepts developed by ancient Greeks! Death by PowerPoint® is often matched in a parallel fashion in written reports.

3. Most word processing programs allow for the insertion of appendix titles and page numbers in the body of a report that will automatically update as they change.

4. There are exceptions, of course. The *9/11 Commission Report*, for example, incorporates narratives because its intended readership includes the American people, who would find them engaging as well as informative: National Commission on Terrorist Attacks. (2004). *9/11 commission report: Final report of the National Commission on Terrorist Attacks upon the United States.* New York: W. W. Norton.

5. It is often the case that a report will go through a number of drafts and be shared with a number of people to get their feedback. In such cases, it is a good idea to include the report's file name and date of last revision or printing in the footer of the cover page. This information will be updated automatically as the report goes through its revisions, and it can be removed with the report's final printing. This is a practice that writers will grow to love.

6. All modern word processors have the capability of scanning for section headings in the report if the headings are properly identified. In Microsoft Word®, for example, first- and lower-order headings can be specified as styles, with each heading given its own label. The same can be done with titles of illustrations, tables or figures, and the like. The key benefit of this is that the word processing program can automatically generate the table of contents inclusive of all headings and their current page locations. Moreover, when changes are made, the program can automatically update the changes into the table of contents. Being able to specify and work with these kind of headings is an ability well worth developing for any writer.

7. As with the headings of sections in the table of contents, the titles used for tables and illustrations in the report can have a style associated with them so that they will automatically be presented in their respective lists with appropriate page numbers.

8. Again, most word processing programs allow for this kind of page linking as with headings in the table of contents.

9. The reference section is usually one of the last sections developed for a project report and, usually, the citations for material used in a project are long gone and forgotten by then. It is important, therefore, to keep a running list of support material as the project moves forward and make sure to centralize it in one location.

Appendix A

Calculating the Critical Path
Using the Critical Path Method

A s the name suggests, the Critical Path Method was designed to help determine the critical path in a network diagram. In addition, it points out the slack in all the tasks that are not on the critical path. The critical path and task slack are determined with a forward and backward pass through the network. For example, Figure A.1 presents Dr. Howard's study given in Chapter 4. Each node in the network is represented by a box. The box contains the task number, name, and time estimate in the upper half. In the lower half of each node are spaces for the earliest and latest start dates for the task and its earliest and latest finish dates.

In Figure A.1, we see the results of a forward pass through the project network. The earliest start date for the first task (3.1, Assemble Test) is 0—the start of the project. Because it will take 3 days to complete, its earliest finish date is 3—three days into the project. All succeeding tasks build on this and other task time requirements. For example, the earliest start date for 3.3, Experiment 2: Stage 1, is Day 3 following the earliest finish date of the task on which it depends. Task 3.3 will take 4 days to complete, so its earliest finish date is 7 days into the project.

Whenever two or more task streams come together, as they do when connecting with 3.8, Analyze Data, the latest "early finish" date of all preceding tasks is chosen for the earliest start date for the succeeding task. It does not matter, for example, that the Stage 2s for Experiments 1 and 3 finish 8 and 6 days into the project. Analyzing Data still cannot begin until Stage 2 of Experiment 2 ends on Day 9—the latest "early finish" date of the three tasks.

This procedure continues until the last task of the project. In Figure A.1, that task is 3.9, Write Report. The earliest it can begin is on Day 13 of the project. It will take 10 days to complete, finishing the project 23 days after it was begun.

The backward pass of the critical path method nails down the critical path and calculates the slack of all noncritical tasks. The backward pass begins with the last day of the last task of the project. Figure A.2 is the same as Figure A.1 except the earliest start and finish dates have been removed for purposes of presentation. The latest finish date for the project's last task is set to its earliest finish date. Now, going backward, task times are subtracted from the project's timeline. The latest start date for Writing Report, for example, must be Day 13 if the project is to be completed by the 23rd day.

When two or more tasks branch out from a task, the latest start date of the task before the branch is given as the latest finish dates to each of them. The second stages of all three experiments, for example, have until Day 9 to finish and still allow Task 3.8, Analyze Data, to begin on time for project completion. This same procedure is followed until the backward pass is complete, ending with the project's first task.

Figure A.3 displays all the information developed on both the forward and backward passes through the project network and indicates the critical path with double-lined arrows. Note that the earliest and latest start and finish dates on the critical path are the same. All of them must start and finish on time or the whole project timeline gets moved. Tasks off the critical path show the slack for each task. For example, Task 3.4, Experiment 3: Stage 1, can start on the 6th day of the project and still finish in time so Stage 2 will not push back the data analysis in Task 3.8.

The critical path method provides a straightforward, commonsense procedure for critical path calculations. The forward pass calculates when the earliest project tasks can begin and end; the backward pass calculates the latest times. When those are the same for any task, it lies on the critical path. When those are different, the task lies off the critical path and provides slack for the project. As projects grow in size and complexity, project management software greatly facilitates these calculations.

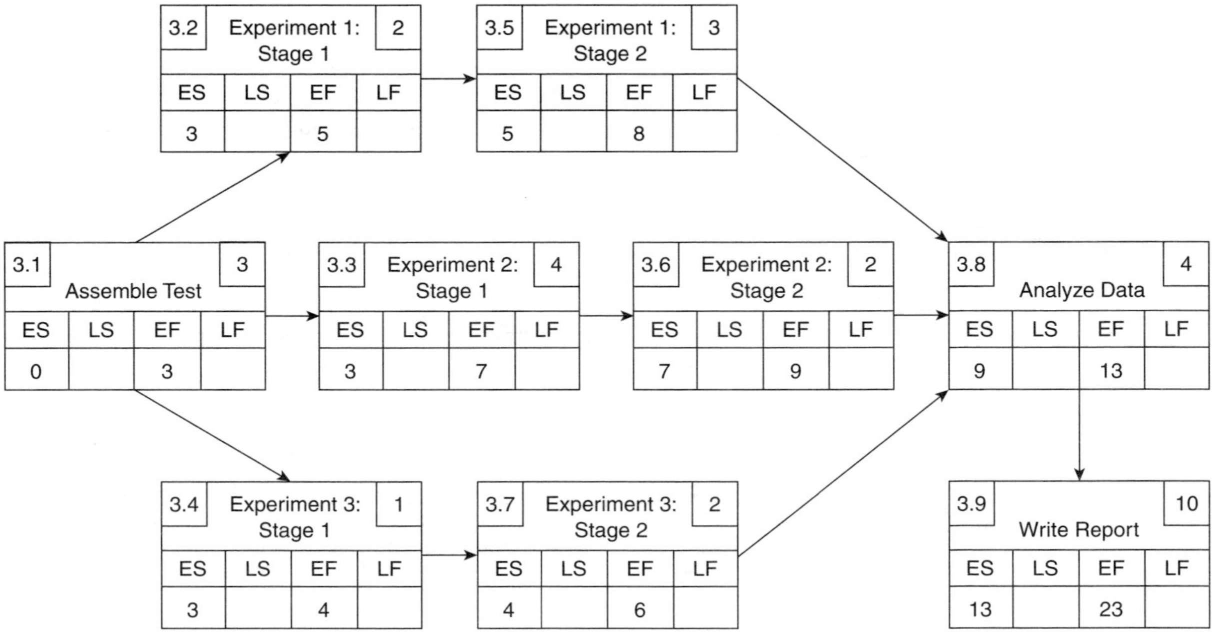

Figure A.1 Dr. Howard's Study—Forward Pass

NOTE: ES = early start; LS = late start; EF = early finish; LF = late finish.

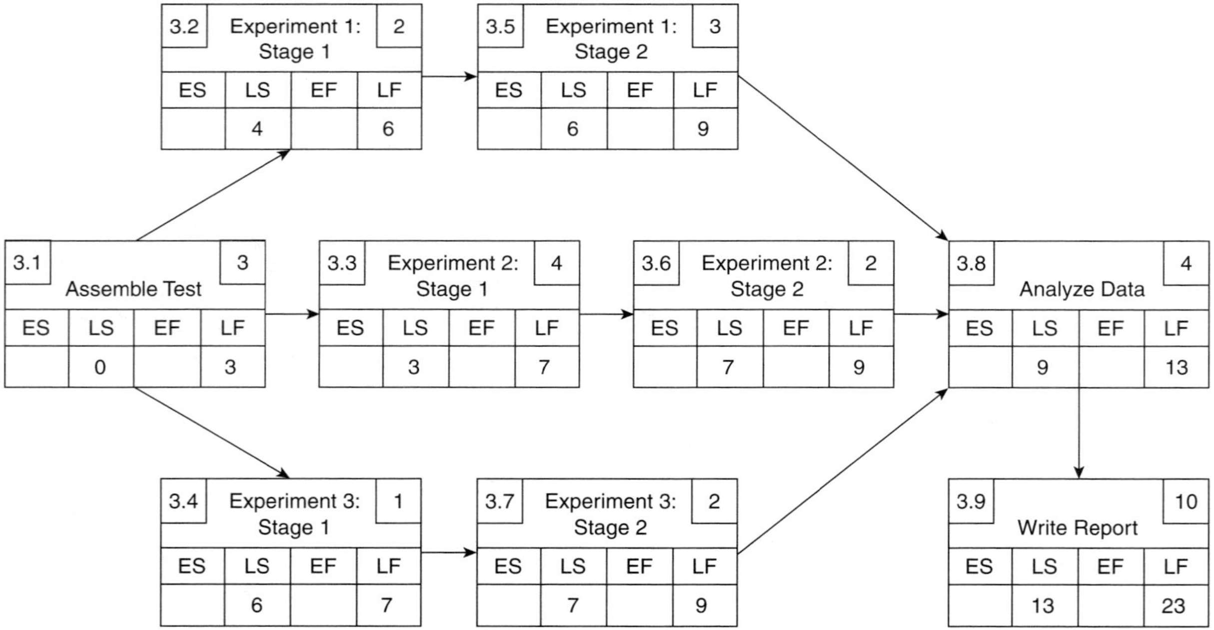

Figure A.2   Dr. Howard's Study—Backward Pass

NOTE: ES = early start; LS = late start; EF = early finish; LF = late finish.

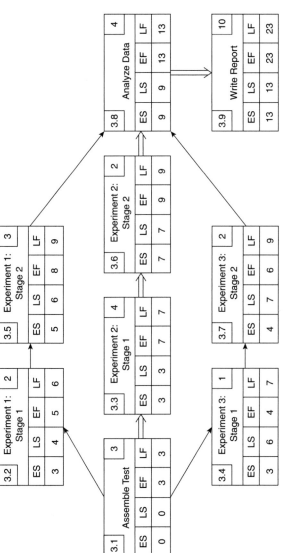

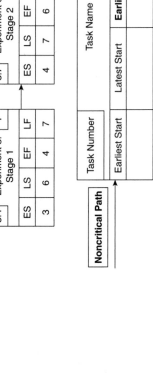

Legend

Figure A.3 Dr. Howard's Study Showing All Start and Finish Dates and the Critical Path

NOTE: ES = early start; LS = late start; EF = early finish; LF = late finish.

163

Appendix B

Earned Value Analysis

Introduction

Earned value analysis is an accounting tool used to help assess the extent to which a project is on schedule and on budget—it marries the time and costs of a project. The components of earned value analysis include planned value, earned value, and actual costs. Planned value and earned value use planned costs to measure the project's progress—the extent to which the project is on schedule or not. They do so by calculating the differences between the money that was planned to be spent by a certain date (planned value) versus the money budgeted for work that was actually completed (earned value). Actual costs versus planned costs are used to assess whether the project is on budget. This is discussed in more detail in the following, starting with the components of planned value, earned value, and actual costs.

- **Planned value:** Planned value refers to the budgeted costs of work scheduled for a project. Recall that in project planning, the costs of all project tasks are estimated and budgeted. The planned value of the project as a whole, then, is the dollar total of all budgeted project tasks.

  At any one point in the life of a project, a certain number of tasks are scheduled to be completed. The planned value of the project to that point is the total dollar value of budgeted tasks that were supposed to be done. The planned value of a project as it proceeds through its life cycle establishes the baseline for the project. It serves as the key reference point for project calculations.

- **Earned value:** Earned value refers to the budgeted cost of work actually performed on a project (not the actual costs—an important distinction). At any point between a project's start and its end, a certain number of tasks will have been completed by that date. The sum total of *budgeted* costs for those completed tasks is that part of the project's planned value that the project has actually earned—its earned value. If the total budgeted costs of work completed are more than the budgeted costs planned for that date, it means that the project is ahead of schedule. (Work is ahead of schedule so the budgeted costs of that work are more than what was planned for by that date.) If the budgeted costs of tasks actually completed are less than planned for by that time, the project is behind schedule (the budgeted costs of tasks done to date are less than the budgeted costs of tasks planned to be done by that date).

- **Actual cost:** The actual cost of a project is the total of all actual costs of work performed in a project by a certain date.

Earned Value Calculations

Earned value calculations use these three figures to help monitor the progress and costs of a project. Earned value versus planned value is a measure of whether the project is ahead of schedule, behind schedule, or on schedule (also known as "schedule variance"). Actual project costs versus earned value (i.e., the budgeted costs of work actually performed) are a measure of whether a project is over, under, or on budget (also known as "cost variance").[1]

Table B.1 shows various earned value calculations for a project that we will use in our discussion. At first, the table can be a little overwhelming. As we go through it, though, the facts and figures begin to fall into place.

For the moment, refer to the upper part of Table B.1. What we see is a Gantt chart of a project with five tasks (1.0–5.0) scheduled to be completed in 11 weeks. On the right side, we see Gantt chart bars showing the schedule for those five tasks. The double line at the end of Week 8 indicates that we are just ending the eighth week of the project. In between the tasks and the chart, we see the budgeted costs for each of the five tasks. For purposes of this example, those costs are distributed equally across the weeks each task is planned to take before completion. The weekly costs for each task are shown in their respective Gantt chart bars.

Just below the Gantt chart bars we see two cost calculations. In the first row are the budgeted costs of work scheduled for each week for all 11 weeks. In the second row, those same costs are added up as the project is scheduled to move forward. Those cumulative costs represent the planned value of the project as it moves through time. Those planned costs serve as a nice point of reference for the project and are referred to as the project's cost baseline. (The bottom of Table B.1 shows figures for several schedule and cost scenarios, which we discuss beginning on page 169.)

Table B.1 Table Showing Budgeted Costs and Actual Cost for a Project with Five Tasks Completed to the Eighth Period of an Eleven Period Project Schedule

Gantt Chart Showing Five Tasks and Budgeted Weekly Costs: Project Is at End of Eighth Week

							Weeks					
Task	Budgeted Costs per Task	1	2	3	4	5	6	7	8	9	10	11
1.0	$4,000	$1,000	$1,000	$1,000	$1,000							
2.0	$2,500			$500	$500	$500	$500	$500				
3.0	$9,000				$1,500	$1,500	$1,500	$1,500	$1,500	$1,500		
4.0	$5,000						$1,000	$1,000	$1,000	$1,000	$1,000	
5.0	$1,500									$500	$500	$500
Budgeted costs of work scheduled for each week		$1,000	$1,000	$1,500	$3,000	$2,000	$3,000	$3,000	$2,500	$3,000	$1,500	$500
Planned Value: Cumulative of budgeted costs of work scheduled—a project's baseline		$1,000	$2,000	$3,500	$6,500	$8,500	$11,500	$14,500	$17,000	$20,000	$21,500	$22,000

(Continued)

Table B.1 (Continued)

Schedule Scenarios: Earned Value Versus Planned Value (see Figure B.1)	Number of Weeks into the Project							
	1	2	3	4	5	6	7	8
Planned Value: Cumulative budgeted costs of work scheduled	$1,000	$2,000	$3,500	$6,500	$8,500	$11,500	$14,500	$17,000
Earned Value: Ahead of schedule	$1,000	$3,000	$5,500	$9,000	$11,500	$16,000	$19,500	$21,000
Schedule variance is positive[a]	$0	$1,000	$2,000	$2,500	$3,000	$4,500	$5,000	$4,000
Earned Value: Behind schedule	$1,000	$1,500	$2,500	$5,000	$6,200	$8,500	$11,000	$13,000
Schedule variance is negative	$0	($500)	($1,000)	($1,500)	($2,300)	($3,000)	($3,500)	($4,000)

Cost Scenarios: Earned Value Versus Actual Costs	Number of Weeks into the Project							
	1	2	3	4	5	6	7	8
Earned Value: Ahead of Schedule (see Figure B.2)	$1,000	$3,000	$5,500	$9,000	$11,500	$16,000	$19,500	$21,000
Actual costs are more than planned	$1,000	$4,000	$6,500	$10,500	$14,000	$19,500	$24,000	$26,500
Cost Variance is negative[b]	$0	$(1,000)	($1,000)	($1,500)	($2,500)	($3,500)	($4,500)	($5,500)
Actual costs are less than planned	$1,000	$2,500	$4,500	$7,500	$10,000	$14,000	$16,500	$18,000
Cost variance is positive	$0	$500	$1,000,	$1,500	$1,500	$2,000	$3,000	$3,000
Earned Value: Behind schedule (see Figure B.3)	$1,000	$1,500	$2,500	$5,000	$6,200	$8,500	$11,000	$13,000
Actual costs are more than planned	$1,000	$1,700	$2,900	$6,000	$6,900	$9,700	$12,500	15,300
Cost variance is negative	$0	$(200)	($400)	($1,000)	$(7,00)	($1,200)	($1,500)	($2,300)
Actual costs are less than planned	$1,000	$1,300	$2,100	$4,200	$5,200	$7,200	$9,500	$11,800
Cost variance is positive	$0	$200	$400	$800	$1,000	$1,300	$1,500	$1,200

a. Schedule variance = earned value – planned value.

b. Cost variance = earned value – actual costs.

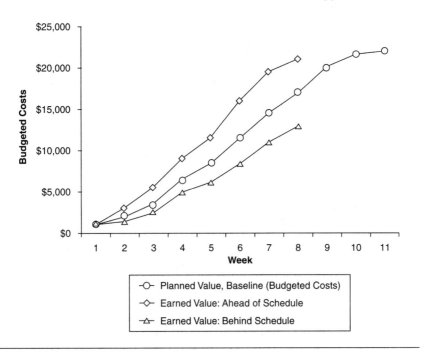

Figure B.1   Earned Value Versus Planned Value (Baseline)

Schedule Variance

Schedule variance is the difference between the earned value of work actually performed and the planned value of work scheduled to be performed (schedule variance = earned value – planned value). A positive variance is usually thought of as good; it means that the work actually performed is ahead of the work scheduled to be performed. A negative variance is usually not so good—the work actually performed is behind the work scheduled to be performed.

Just below the Gantt chart in the bottom part of Table B.1 we see "Schedule Scenarios: Earned Value Versus Planned Value." The first scenario shows what happens when tasks are done sooner than expected—the budgeted costs of those tasks rise faster than planned. This results in positive figures for the earned value of the project (i.e., a positive variance). The second scenario shows what happens when tasks are done later than expected—the budgeted costs of the tasks rise slower than planned. This results in negative figures for earned value. Both of these scenarios are shown in Figure B.1, "Earned Value Versus Planned Value (Baseline)." The graph shows how these positive and negative values for earned value compare to the project's baseline of planned value.

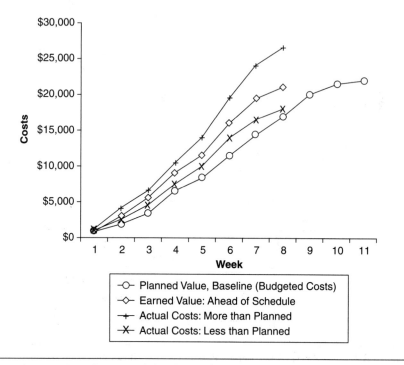

Figure B.2   Actual Costs While Ahead of Schedule

Cost Variance

Cost variance—the extent to which the project is over or under budget—compares actual costs to earned value—not planned value. We use earned value because if the project were ahead of schedule, we would expect the actual costs to be more than what was planned because the work actually performed is ahead of what was planned. If the project were behind schedule, on the other hand, we would expect actual costs to be less than what was planned.

Below the "Schedule Scenarios" in Table B.1 are the "Cost Scenarios: Earned Value Versus Actual Costs." The first set of cost scenarios show actual costs when the actual work done (earned value) is ahead of schedule. The first row shows the earlier figures for earned value when the project is ahead of schedule. They are more than the planned value figures at the bottom of the Gantt chart, indicating the project is ahead of plans. The next two rows show actual costs running more than planned for the work completed and then the resulting negative cost figures (i.e., negative cost variance). Here the project is over budget but ahead of schedule. The next two rows show actual costs running less than planned and a positive cost variance. Here the project is ahead of schedule and under budget—a nice position to be in! Figure B.2, "Actual

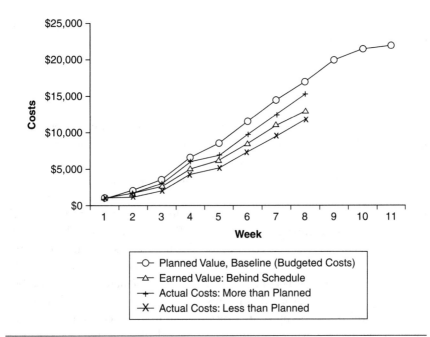

Figure B.3   Actual Costs While Behind Schedule

Costs While Ahead of Schedule," shows those scenarios graphically. Figure B.2 has the same baseline as Figure B.1 and the same earned value line that shows the project ahead of schedule. We have added to it actual costs illustrating a project over and under budget.

The second set of cost scenarios show actual costs when the work done is behind schedule. The first row shows the earlier figures for earned value when the project was behind schedule. The next two rows show actual costs to be more than planned and then the figures indicating a negative cost variance. The project is over budget and now behind schedule—not a great position! The other two rows show actual costs less than planned with a positive cost variance. The project is under budget but still behind schedule. Figure B.3, "Actual Costs While Behind Schedule," shows those scenarios graphically with the same baseline and "behind schedule" earned value as in Figure B.1. We have added actual costs that represent a project over and under budget to it.

Uses of Earned Value Analysis

Earned value analysis provides a quick method to signal when projects are ahead, behind, or on schedule and over, under, or on budget. Just when those signals become red flags and how to interpret and respond to them are managerial decisions.

Caveats

The managerial utility of earned value analysis must take into consideration a number of issues about the calculations themselves. First, the calculations are based on dollars spent. Dollars spent may or may not represent actual work done. Consider, for example, Dr. Howard's project in Chapter 4. Dr. Howard was putting together a rather high-tech laboratory for his research work on bio-informatics. Some tasks called for the installation of high-tech (and very costly) equipment. When that equipment is received, it can be charged against the planned costs of the installation task. If the equipment costs, say, $1,000,000, and the labor to install it costs $10,000 but will take a month to finish once begun, you can see an immediate problem. Earned value analysis could indicate that the task is more than 99% complete simply on the arrival of the equipment. Rules of thumb are used to address what might be considered arbitrary and misleading calculations like this. One rule is to charge 50% of planned value once a task has begun; another is to hold off until the entire task is complete. The effect of such rules, however, can also be arbitrary and misleading.[2]

Other problems in earned value analysis come from how people will try to manipulate the figures. When actual costs are calculated and charged to a project or when a task is designated as begun or ended can make significant differences in earned value calculations. Although all this seems to smack of dishonesty, honest differences in opinion often occur. Project personnel are not the only people who might want to adjust the figures in earned value calculations. Client representatives may have agendas of their own (both positive or negative) that affect how earned value analyses are calculated and then shown to higher management in the client organization.

These and other problems simply point out that there are limitations in what earned value analysis can and cannot do for project leaders. Like any management tool, earned value analysis has value when used with care.

Endnotes

1. Discussion of earned value analysis is limited here to schedule and cost variance.

2. Accounting rules are also available to account for equipment charges and the like. As one can imagine, these rules can become quite complex quickly.

Index

Achievement Project, 82, 102
  end users/implementers of, 108
  political stakeholders and, 108–109
  social capital and, 110–113,
    110–112 (figures)
  stakeholder expectations and, 84
  team structural fundamentals and, 86–92
  See also Project teams; Stakeholders
Adjourning process, 5, 94–95, 96–97,
  132–133, 137
Analogous budgeting, 27, 32, 47
Authority for decisions, 26, 32, 52–53

Backward pass. *See* Critical Path Method
  (CPM)
Baltimore Project, 14–15
  costs of, 27
  mission statement for, 19–20
  objectives/deliverables and, 22–24,
    23–24 (table), 24–25 (figure)
  project report and, 146
  scope of, 26
  timeline in, 27–28
  See also Initiation stage
Bar charts, 62, 63–65 (figures)
Bio-Informatics Project, 60–61
  components of scheduling and, 63, 66–68
  Critical Path Method and, 62–63,
    66 (figure), 159–160,
    161–162 (figures)
  dependencies of tasks and, 69–70
  Earned Value Analysis and, 172
  Gantt/bar chart techniques and, 62,
    63–65 (figures), 69
  network of tasks and, 70–71
  work breakdown structure and, 69
  See also Scheduling
Blanchard, K. H., 133, 134
Bottom-up budgeting, 27, 42, 47
Budgeting. *See* Costs; Earned Value Analysis

Charter, 28–30, 29 (table), 32
China Report, 142, 148, 151
Clients, 17, 21, 103–105
Closing phase. *See* Adjourning process
Cold Calls, 26
Communication technology, 88–89
Competitive strategy, 2
Compliance Project, 38–39
  organizational structure and, 42–43,
    50, 52
  project administration and, 46
  project report for, 146, 147
  resource estimation, 48
  work breakdown structure in, 39–41,
    40–41 (figure)
Costs, 5, 26, 27, 32
  analysis of, 130
  bottom-up budgeting and, 27, 42, 47
  estimation of, 50, 51 (table)
  top-down/analogous budgeting and, 27,
    32, 47
  See also Earned Value Analysis;
    Resource allocation
Critical Path Method (CPM), 62–63,
  66 (figure), 68–69, 70–71,
  159–161, 161–162 (figures)

Decision making:
  authority for, 26, 32, 52–53
  expert advisors and, 146
  project reports and, 144–146
  See also Project leaders; Project
    management
Deliverables. *See* Objectives/
  deliverables

Earned Value Analysis, 75, 130, 165
  actual cost and, 166
  calculations in, 166–172,
    167–168 (table)

cost variance, 170–171,
    170–171 (figures)
earned value and, 165–166
planned value and, 165
schedule variance and, 169,
    169 (figure)
utility of, 171–172
End users, 18, 103, 108,
    115, 146–147
Entry-level project skills, 3
Execution stage, 5, 94, 96,
    108, 115–116
project leadership and, 129–132
project reports and, 146–147
project teams and, 129–131
See also Launch stage
Expert advisors, 146

Face-to-face interaction, 88–89
Float, 68, 70–71
Forward pass. See Critical Path Method
    (CPM)
Free riding, 75, 86

Gantt charts, 62,
    63–65 (figures), 69
Goal specification process, 21, 22–24,
    23–24 (table), 24–25 (figure), 92

Hersey, P., 133, 134
Host organizations, 17–18, 27, 105,
    115, 131
Human resources, 26, 32, 48, 84

Implementation. See Execution stage
Individual project members, 133–134
Information resource, 26, 32
Initiation stage, 4, 15
    authority for decisions and, 26, 32
    costs of, 27, 32
    human resources and, 26, 32
    information resource and, 26, 32
    mission statement, 16–19, 31
    project charter and, 29–30,
        29 (table)
    project leadership and, 126–127
    project objectives/deliverables and,
        20–22, 32
    project plan, elements of, 30–31
    scope of the project, 25–26
    stakeholders in, 17–19, 20, 22, 31–32
    timeline in, 27–28, 32

See also Baltimore Project; Launch stage;
    Planning stage; Work breakdown
    structure (WBS)

Johnson, D. E., 133, 134

Katzenbach, J. R., 83, 95

Lag time, 67
Launch stage, 5, 127–128, 136
Leadership. See Project leaders;
    Project management
Lead time, 67
Lockwood, D. L., 121
Luthans, F., 121

Milestone events, 67
Mintzberg, H., 121
Mission statement, 16, 31
    clients and, 17
    definition/role of, 16–17
    end users and, 18
    host organizations and, 17–18
    political role of, 17
    project direction and, 16–17
    project teams and, 18
    stakeholders and, 17–19, 31–32
    suppliers and, 18–19
    See also Initiation stage
Monte Carlo simulations, 63

Networks, 26
    project leaders and, 122
    project tasks, interrelatedness of, 68,
        70–71
    social capital networks, 109–114,
        110–112 (figures), 116
    See also Stakeholders

Objectives/deliverables, 20, 32
    clients and, 21, 104
    definition of, 21
    roles of, 21–22
    SMART objectives and, 22, 53, 56
    stakeholder agreement and, 22
    team direction and, 21–22, 84
    See also Baltimore Project; Initiation
        stage; Project teams; Stakeholders
Organizational processes, 2, 42–43

PERT (Project Evaluation and Review
    Technique) scheduling, 49, 63

Planning stage, 4–5
  project charter and, 28–30,
    29 (table), 32
  project leadership and, 126–127
  project plan, elements of,
    30–31, 33
  project structure, development of, 50–54,
    54 (table)
  See also Initiation stage; Scheduling;
    Work breakdown structure (WBS)
Political elements:
  mission statements and, 17
  political players, 108–109, 116
Problem-solver role, 124, 130–131,
  136–137
Product development, 2
Project Evaluation and Review Technique
  (PERT) scheduling, 49, 63
Project leaders, 5–6, 120–121, 134
  adjourning process and,
    132–133, 137
  champion/negotiator roles and,
    122–123, 135
  coordinator role and, 124
  directive vs. participatory leadership
    and, 137
  execution stage and, 129–132, 136–137
  external stakeholders and,
    131–132, 137
  figurehead/spokesperson roles
    and, 121–122, 134
  individual project members and,
    133–134
  initiation/planning stages and, 126–127,
    135–136
  launch stage and, 127–128, 136
  leadership positions,
    assignment of, 52–53
  liaison/monitor roles and, 122, 134–135
  objectives/deliverables,
    determination of, 104
  planner/resource allocator
    roles and, 123–124
  problem-solver role and, 124, 130–131,
    136–137
  project control role and,
    123, 135
  project life cycle and, 126–133, 135–137
  project structure, development of, 50,
    52–54, 54 (table)
  promotions and, 120
  resource estimation and, 48

  roles of, 121–125, 134–135
  schedules, revision/modification of,
    74–75
  team leader role and, 124–125, 129–131
  See also Project management; Project
    teams; Stakeholders; Work
    breakdown structure (WBS)
Project life cycle, 4
  closing phase, 5
  execution stage, 5
  initiation stage, 4
  launch stage, 5
  planning stage, 4–5
  project leadership roles and, 126–133,
    135–137
  team role assignment and, 91
Project management, 2, 3
  goal specification process, 21, 22–24,
    23–24 (table), 24–25 (figure), 92
  political stakeholders and,
    108–109
  project administration and, 45–46
  social-psychological dimension
    of, 6, 86
  task dimensions of, 5–6
  See also Project leaders; Project teams;
    Work breakdown
    structure (WBS)
Project Management Institute, 39
Project mind-set, 2
Project reports, 142–143, 155
  appendices in, 146, 153, 156
  back end material in, 153
  body of, 150–153
  components of, 147–153, 154 (table),
    155–156
  conclusions/ recommendations
    section in, 152
  cover page in, 148
  decision-makers and, 144–146
  end users/implementers and, 146–147
  executive summary in, 149–150
  expert advisors and, 146
  front end material in, 148–150
  introduction for, 150–151
  letter of transmittal for, 148
  lists of tables/illustrations and, 149
  readership considerations and, 143–147
  references/bibliography section
    in, 153
  sections/subsections of, 151
  table of contents in, 149

Project team environment.
  See Stakeholders
Project teams, 2–3, 18, 83–84, 105–106
  adjourning process, 94–95, 96–97
  commitment/satisfaction in,
    85–86, 88
  composition of, 86–87
  developmental needs of, 85
  direction of, 21–22, 84, 92
  effective teams, characteristics of,
    84–86, 95–96
  execution stage and, 129–131
  formation stage of, 92–93, 96
  governance issues in, 87–88
  ideology, commonalities
    in, 89–92
  interaction, modes of, 88–89
  norms of, 90, 94, 96
  performance stage of, 94, 96
  project leaders and, 124–125, 129–131
  size of, 86
  storming stage, disagreements
    and, 93–94, 96
  synergy in, 83
  task roles in, 90–91
  team identity formation and, 88
  See also Achievement Project; Individual
    project members; Project leaders;
    Stakeholders
Projects:
  charters of, 28–30, 29 (table), 32
  leadership dimensions and, 5–6
  life cycles of, 4–5
  mission statements and, 16–19
  objective/deliverables and,
    20–24, 23–24 (table),
    24–25 (figure)
  parameters of, 5, 25–28
  project plans, elements of, 30–31, 33
  unique nature of, 3–4
  See also Project reports; Project teams;
    Stakeholders

Quality circles, 2

Regulatory responsibilities,
    107, 115
Relationship-building. See Social
    capital; Stakeholders
Reports. See Project reports
Resource allocation, 25–26
  estimation of resources, 48–49

  overuse of resources, 74–75
  project leaders and, 123–124
  realignment of resources, 74–75
  resource mathematics, 75, 86
  suppliers and, 106–107
  See also Costs; Earned Value Analysis

Scheduling, 61, 76 (table)
  adjustments to, 74–75, 78
  assumptions/estimates, revision of,
    73–74, 78
  components of schedules, 63, 66–68, 77–78
  Critical Path Method and, 62–63,
    66 (figure), 68, 70–71,
    159–163, 161–162 (figures)
  dependencies of tasks and, 67, 69–70, 73
  Gantt/bar chart techniques, 62,
    63–65 (figures), 69
  lag/lead times and, 67
  milestone events and, 67
  network of tasks and, 68, 70
  PERT scheduling, 49, 66
  project command/control and, 75, 77–78
  schedule development process, 69–71
  slack/float and, 68, 70–71
  stakeholders and, 72–73
  task clusters, project
    phases and, 72
  tasks/activities and, 66
  time estimates, review of, 69
  types of schedules, 61–66, 77
  whole-project visualization and,
    71–73, 78
  work breakdown structure and,
    69, 77–78
  See also Earned Value Analysis; Planning
    stage; Project teams
Scope of a project, 5, 25–26
  scope creep and, 104
  work breakdown structure and, 46
Situational leadership theory, 133–134
Slack, 68, 70
SMART (specific/measurable/
    actionable/realistic/time
    delimited) objectives, 22, 53, 56
Smith, D. K., 83, 95
Social capital, 109, 116
  development of, 113–114
  nature of, 110–113, 110–112 (figures)
Social-psychological dimension, 6, 86
Stakeholders, 31–32, 102, 103, 114–116
  clients, 17, 21, 103–105

end users/implementers and, 108
expectations of, 84, 104
host organizations and, 17–18,
    27, 105
mission statements and, 17–19
objectives/deliverables and, 20,
    22, 45
political players and, 108–109
project leaders and, 131–132
project overview and, 73
regulators/inspectors and, 107
suppliers, 18–19, 106–107
See also Achievement project; Project
    leaders; Project teams; Social capital
Standard operating procedures (SOPs), 38,
    39–40, 45
Suppliers, 18–19, 106–107, 115

Tasks, 5–6, 66
clusters, project phases/subcomponents
    and, 72
critical sequencing and, 68–69
dependencies and, 66–67, 69–70, 72
lag/lead times and, 67
milestones and, 68
networks of , 68
project teams, task roles in, 90–91
slack/float and, 68
Teams. *See* Project teams
Technology for communication, 88–89
Timeline, 5, 27–28, 32
critical sequence of tasks
    and, 68
lag/lead time, 67

slack/float and, 68
task dependencies and, 66–67
time requirements, estimation of,
    49–50, 69
Top-down budgeting, 27, 32, 47
Traditional project work, 2, 5–6
host organizations and, 17–18
See also Projects

Virtual Teams, 88–89

Work breakdown structure
    (WBS), 39–41, 40–41 (figure),
    54 (table)
back loading and, 53
core tasks in, 43–44
costs, estimation of, 50, 51 (table)
development process for, 43–46
organizational structure development
    and, 42–43
project administration and, 45–46
project planning and, 44–45
project structure, development of, 50,
    52–54
resources, estimation of, 48–49
roles of, 41–43
scope of project work and, 42
support tasks in, 44–46
time requirements, estimation of, 49–50
top-down vs. bottom-up estimation
    and, 42, 47–48
See also Compliance Project;
    Project teams; Scheduling
Writing. *See* Project reports

About the Author

Anthony T. (Terry) Cobb is an Associate Professor of Management at Virginia Tech. Dr. Cobb received his master's degree in urban planning from Wayne State University in Michigan and his Ph.D. in administration from the University of California at Irvine. Dr. Cobb first began project work for the Public Policy Research Organization during his Ph.D. program and rose to the level of project manager. Dr. Cobb teaches a wide variety of management courses and integrates project management and team training into all of them. Dr. Cobb has worked for, consulted with, and trained personnel for a variety of organizations, making use of project management tools and skills and training others in their use.